REVOLUTIONARY
PENSIONERS
OF
1818

MESSAGE

FROM

THE PRESIDENT OF THE UNITED STATES,

TRANSMITTING

A REPORT

OF

THE SECRETARY OF WAR,

IN

COMPLIANCE WITH A RESOLUTION OF THE SENATE,

" To cause to be laid before them, a list of all the Pensioners of the United States, the sum annually paid to each, and the States or Territories in which the said Pensioners are respectively paid."

MARCH 28, 1818.
Printed by order of the Senate of the United States.

CLEARFIELD

Originally published
Washington, D.C., 1818

Reprinted for
Clearfield Company, Inc. by
Genealogical Publishing Co., Inc.
Baltimore, Maryland
1991, 1992, 1996, 1998

International Standard Book Number: 0-8063-0351-4

INDEX TO STATES

To the Senate of the United States:

In compliance with a resolution of the Senate, relative to the pensioners of the United States, the sum annually paid to each, and the states or territories in which the said pensioners are respectively paid, I now transmit a report, from the Secretary of War, which, with documents marked A and B, contain all the information required.

JAMES MONROE.

Washington, March 28, 1818.

Department of War, March 24, 1818.

The Secretary of War, to whom was referred the resolution of the Senate, requesting the President of the United States "To cause to be laid before them, a list of all the pensioners of the United States, the sum annually paid to each, and the states or territories in which the said pensioners are respectively paid" has the honor to report the documents marked A and B.

J. C. CALHOUN,

The President of the United States.

A.

LIST of *Invalid Pensioners* of the United States, belonging to the State of *New Hampshire, and paid at Portsmouth, New Hampshire, with the annual allowance to each annexed, viz:*

		per annum.
Peter Akerman	Private	At $64
Andrew Aikin	Sergeant Major	72
Caleb Aldrich	Sergeant	96
Caleb Austin	Private	32
Samuel Allen	Ditto	38 40
Theophilus B. Adams	Corporal	48
Enoch Abbott	Private	48
Daniel Buzzle	Ditto	90
Archelaus Batchelor	Sergeant	48
Ebenezer Bean	Private	48
Francis Blood	Ditto	96
John V. Barron	1st Lieutenant	153
Jeremiah Bean	Private	48
Zachariah Bunker	Ditto	95
Seth Bisbee	Corporal	48
William Burbeck	Private	48
James Bean, Jun.	Corporal	32
Benjamin Brown	Private	32
James Campbell	Ditto	77 80
Nathaniel Church	Ditto	96
Ebenezer Carleton	Ditto	96

A.—Continued.

Name			Rank			At $72 per annum.
Levi Chubbock			Fifer			24
Morril Coburn			Private			24
William Curtis			Ditto			96
James Crummitt			Ditto			96
Jabez Church			Ditto			48
Benjamin Cotton			Ditto			48
Josiah Chandler			Ditto			48
William Crawford			Ditto			72
James Cook			Ditto			32
Othaniel Cross			Corporal			96
Joseph Cillery			Brevet captain			240
Joseph Colbath			Corporal			24
Jonathan Clark			Ditto			48
Joshua Chesley			Ditto			24
James Chesley			Private			48
David Duncan			Ditto			64
Henry Danforth			Ditto			48
James Dean			Ditto			24
Lemuel Dean			Ditto			96
Francis Davidson			Ditto			76 80
James Dow			Musician			96
Edward Evans			Private			96

A.—Continued.

Name	Rank	At $72 per annum.
Thomas Eastman	Private	
Jonathan Elkins	Ditto	32
John Elliott -	Ditto	64
Ebenezer Fletcher	Fifer	24
Stephen Fuller	Private	32
David Fowler -	Ditto	32
Robert Friend	Ditto	96
Edward Fettch	Ditto	32
Joseph Foy -	Sergeant	96
James Gould -	Lieutenant	181 32
Moses S. George	Private	48
Joshua Gilman	Ditto	64
Windsor Gleason	Ditto	24
Joseph Grooley	Ditto	24
Joseph Green	Ditto	48
Jonas Green -	Ditto	96
Moses Gilman	Ditto	48
William Gardner	Ditto	24
William Hastings	Ditto	96
Thomas Haynes	Ditto	96
Joshua Haynes	Ditto	76 80
Nathan Holt -	Ditto	24

2

A.—Continued.

Name	Rank	At $48 per annum.
Charles Himtoon, jun.	Private	48
Zadock Hurd	Ditto	82
Joseph Hilton	Lieutenant	90 66
Jonathan Holton	Ditto	136
James Hawkley	Private	96
Ephraim Hall	Ditto	72
Obid S. Hatch	Sergeant	96
Joseph Hacket	Private	96
William Haines	Corporal	48
Robert M. C. Holmes	Private	96
Nathaniel Hoyt	Ditto	48
Ebenezer Jennings	Sergeant	24
Peter Johnson	Private	24
James Ervine	Ditto	72
Abraham Kimball	Ditto	48
Benjamin Knight	Sergeant	32
John Knight	Private	48
Samuel Lacount	Ditto	96
Samuel Lathrop	Ditto	96
John Lapish	Ditto	24
Nathaniel Leavitt	Corporal	96
John Lincoln	Private	57 46

A.—Continued.

		At $96 per annum.
Joshua Lovejoy	Sergeant	96
Nehemiah Leavitt	Corporal	48
Randall M'Allister	Private	96
Andrew M'Gaffy	Lieutenant	139 66
Noah Marsh	Private	32
Joseph Morrell	Ditto	96
Jonathan Margeny	Ditto	64
James Moore	Ditto	96
Samuel Morrell	Ditto	72
Joseph Moss	Private	64
Seymour Marsh	Ditto	48
Josiah Moor	Ditto	32
William Moody	Ditto	96
Benjamin Marston	Ditto	32
David M'Duffee	Ditto	72
Jonathan Nute	Sergeant	96
Benjamin Neally	Ditto	64
John Orr	Lieutenant	136
Phineas Parkhurst	Fifer	96
Joel Porter	Private	24
Samuel Potter	Sergeant	64
Asa Putney	Ditto	48

A.—Continued.

Name	Rank	per annum.
Joseph Patterson	Private	At $48
Jonathan Perkins	Ensign	78
William Powers	Private	48
John S. Pevey	Ditto	96
John Purington	Ditto	32
David Pratt	Sergeant	72
Thomas Pillsbury	Private	64
Joseph W. Page	Sergeant	48
John Reed	Private	96
Stephen Richardson	Ditto	38 40
Daniel Russell	Ditto	96
Charles Rice	Ditto	48
Noah Robinson	Lieutenant	136
Joseph Richardson	Private	48
Jonathan Richards	Ditto	48
Benjamin Robinson	Ditto	32
Jonathan Redman	Ditto	19 20
Stephen N. Rand	Ditto	48
John Rendall	Ditto	96
Joseph Slack	Ditto	64
John Sam. Sherburne	Major	300
Thomas Simpson	Lieutenant	181 32

A.—Continued.

Name	Rank	per annum.
Aaron Smith	Ensign	At $156
Noah Sinclair	Private	72
John Simpson	Ditto	64
Reuben Spencer	Ditto	64
Amos Stafford	Ditto	64
Hezekiah Sawtell	Ditto	48
Samuel Sterns	Ditto	48
William Smart	Ditto	96
Charles Stickney	Ditto	48
Benjamin Stevenson	Second lieutenant	135
William St. Clair	Sergeant	96
Elisha Smith	Private	96
Jeremiah Towle	Corporal	51 20
Moses Trussell	Private	96
Ebenezer Tinkham	Ditto	48
William Taggart	Ensign	78
Nathan Taylor	Lieutenant	136
James Trowbridge	Sergeant	64
Lemuel Traston	Private	96
Jonathan Wilkins	Marine	48
William Wallace	Private	96
William Wood	Ditto	64

A.—Continued.

		per annum.
Weymouth Wallace	Private	At £48
Josiah Walton	Ditto	32
Jacob Wilman, jun.	Ditto	24
Francis Whitcomb	Ditto	32
Robert B. Wilkins	Ditto	96
Seth Wyman	Ditto	76 80
Edward Waldo	Lieutenant	138 66
Jonathan Willard	Ensign	156
Samuel Wells	Sergeant	72
Frederick Wilkins	Private	96
Silas Whitcomb	Ditto	52
Bela Young	Sergeant	84

Making 164 for New Hampshire.

A.—Continued.

LIST *of Invalid Pensioners of the United States, belonging to the State of Massachusetts, and paid at Boston, with the annual allowance to each annexed—viz:*

Name	Rank	per annum.
George Airs	Matross	At $80
Caleb Atherton	Private	64
John Adams	Ditto	64
Aaron Abbott	Ditto	42 65¾
Malachi Allen	Ditto	32
Luke Aldridge	Ditto	48
Gustavus Aldrick	Sergeant	96
Spafford Ames	Private	96
Robert Ames	Ditto	96
Isaac Abbott	Lieutenant	108 80
Thomas Aspinwall	Lieutenant Colonel by brevet	360
Michael Acorn	Private	48
John Allen	Ditto	48
Ira Averill	Corporal	57 60
Henry Allen	Private	96
Ebenezer T. Adams	Ditto	48
George Ayres	Ditto	72

A.—Continued.

Name	Rank	At $24 per annum.
Nehemiah Adams	Private	24
Ebenezer Bancroft	Captain	72
John Bryant	Lieutenant	204
Elias Barron	Dragoon	96
Joseph Brown	Sergeant	96
Jonathan Ball	Ditto	68 80
Perez Bradford	Ditto	38 40
Nathaniel Bowen	Ditto	96
John Barberie	Corporal	96
John Bean	Ditto	64
Benjamin Berry	Private	96
Abner Briggs	Ditto	96
Phineas Butler	Ditto	96
Peter Barrows	Ditto	44 80
Jonas Bladgett	Ditto	64
Nathaniel Baker	Ditto	64
Squire Bishop, jun.	Ditto	64
Josiah Ball	Ditto	42 65¾
George Bacon	Ditto	76 80
Ephraim Bailey	Ditto	96
Robert Bancroft	Ditto	16

A.—Continued.

Name	Rank	At $24 per annum.
James Batcheldore	Private	96
John Berry	Ditto	96
Elijah Brainard	Ditto	96
Ebenezer Brown	Sergeant	96
George Blood	Private	32
Ebenezer Balkcom	Corporal	96
John Bennet	Private	64
Jonathan Bates	Ditto	57 60
Jonathan Brown	Ditto	32
William Babcock	Ditto	48
Mark Barter	Ditto	96
Joseph Barter	Ditto	48
Jonathan Brown	Ditto	19 20
William Brown	Ditto	96
Jeremiah Bettis	Sergeant	48
Robert Boyle	Private	48
Luther Brittain	Ditto	96
Nicholas Bartlett	Ditto	72
Noah Butts	Ditto	96
William Blanchard	Ditto	48
Levi Beals	Artificer	

3

A.—Continued.

Name	Rank	At $32	per annum.
John Bickford	Private	6⅔	
Augustus Ballow	Ditto	96	
Samuel Baker	Ditto	64	
Josiah Chute	Sergeant	42	65⅜
Abel Carpenter	Ditto	96	
Jonas Childs	Private	96	
Job Caswell	Ditto	6⅔	
Timothy Chase	Ditto	64	
William Conant	Ditto	64	
Moses Cass	Ditto	96	
Levi Chadburne	Ditto	42	65⅜
Solomon Cole	Ditto	2⅔	
Noah Clough	Ditto	24	
Nathan Cook	Ditto	96	
Richard Crouch	Ditto	24	
James Campbell	Ditto	24	
Caleb Chadwick	Ditto	32	
Barnabas Chapman	Ditto	48	
Richard Chase	Ditto	64	
Joseph Coxe	Sergeant	64	
Thomas Crowell	Private	96	

A.—Continued.

		per annum.
George Cammell	Private	At $48
John Careton	Ditto	48
Henry Carver	Ditto	96
William Clarke	Ditto	48
William Cushing	Lieutenant	136
Isaac Campbell	Private	48
Timothy Cook	Corporal	72
Ebenezer Cobb	Ditto	96
Amos G Corey	Private	48
Isaac Crossman	Ditto	48
James Carlton	Ditto	48
Leighton Colbath	Ditto	48
Thomas Cochrane	Ditto	48
Cal b Critchet	Ditto	48
Isaac Carver	Ditto	48
Richard Cummings	Ditto	32
Joseph Carr	Ditto	19 20
John Crampersey	Ditto	480
Isaac Connery	Ditto	24
Charles Chase	Ditto	48
Clark Case	Ditto	96

A.—Continued.

		At £48 per annum.
Samuel S. Clark	Sergeant	At £48
Daniel Collomy	Private	48
Nathan Crosby	Ditto	48
William Cummings	Ditto	24
Ebenezer Childs	Captain	240
Artemas Conant	Private	64
Joseph Currill	Ditto	64
Alexander Campbell	Sergeant	72
Ebenezer Cobb	Corporal	96
Seth Delano	Sergeant	51 20
Thomas Doty	Private	96
Jonathan Davis	Ditto	48
John Duncan	Ditto	42 65¾
Jerathmiel Doty	Marine	53 31¼
David Dunning	Corporal of artillery	48
Sylvester Dean	Private	96
Elisha Demming	Ditto	48
Samuel Day	Sergeant	64
William Decoster	Private	48
Frank Dunnehill	Ditto	48
William Darrell	Ditto	84

A.—Continued.

Name	Rank	At $96 per annum.
Daniel Door	Private	96
Robert Elwell	Bombadier	96
William Earl	Marine	96
John Edgerly	Private	72
Abner Egleston	Ditto	48
Samuel Ensworth	Ditto	64
Thomas Entwisle	Sergeant	57 60
William Eastman	Private	80
Henry Farwell	Captain	120
Jonas Farnsworth	Ditto	96
John Francis	Private	76 80
William Foster	Sergeant	64
Samuel Fowle	Private	64
Jedediah Fuller	Ditto	48
Levi Farnsworth	Ditto	19 20
Moses Fitch	Ditto	48
Frederick Follet	Ditto	12
Joseph Frost	Ditto	80
Benjamin Farnham	Captain	64
Thomas Foot	Private	72
Albert Fowler	Corporal	

A.—Continued.

Name	Rank	At $72 per annum.
Levi Farnsworth	Private	96
Phinas Frost	Ditto	64
John Fuller	Ditto	64
Benjamin Fuller	Ditto	48
Joseph Fritts	Ditto	48
Aaron W. Forbush	Sergeant	48
Judson Farrer	Private	96
Gardner Foster	Sergeant	96
John Gould	Private	96
Jonathan Gleason	Ditto	64
Silas Gill	Ditto	52
Samuel Green	Ditto	16
Isaac Green	Ditto	96
Henry Gates	Ditto	24
Uriah Goodwin	Ditto	76 80
Deborah Gannett	Ditto	48
Charles Gowin	Ditto	72
Edward Grantt	Ditto	57 60
James Gallut	Ditto	48
William Gunnison	Ditto	72
Rufus Goodnoy	Dito	

A.—Continued.

Name	Rank	At $64 per annum.
John Goff, jun.	Private	64
John Glover	Ditto	6½
Alexander Gardner	Ditto	96
Zachariah Godfrey	Ditto	24
Benjamin Gilbreth	Sergeant	96
Luther Gregory	Private	48
William Gleason	Ditto	48
Benjamin Glover	Sergeant	32
Harvey Gaylard	Private	48
Elijah Hudson	Sergeant	76 80
Solomon Hayward	Ditto	76 80
Daniel Horn	Ditto	32
John Hicks	Private	96
Daniel Hickey	Ditto	96
Peter Hopkins	Ditto	64
Joseph Handy	Ditto	48
Josiah Howard	Ditto	42 65½
Daniel Hemmenway	Ditto	32
William Hubbard	Marine	96
Gamaliel Handy	Private	64
Peter Hemmenway	Ditto	96

A.—Continued.

Name	Rank	At $12 per annum.
Jesse Holt	Corporal	48
Ambrose Homan	Private	48
Caleb Hopkins	Ditto	96
Robert Hall	Ditto	96
Thomas Harrison	Major	300
John Hair	Private	48
Francis Hagar	Ditto	96
James Hatch	Ditto	48
Andrew Hall	Ditto	82
Isaac Hawland	Ditto	82
David Hoar	Ditto	48
Benjamin Haskell	Ditto	82
John Haskell	Ditto	96
Joel Horsham	Ditto	72
Daniel Henderson	First lieutenant	186
James Howard	Private	72
Benjamin Hotten	Ditto	96
Ithram Harris	Sergeant	64
John Hill	Private	96
James Harrington	Ditto	72
William Jacobs	Ditto	96

A—Continued.

		At 8 96 per annum.
Joseph Johnson	Private	96
Josiah Jones, 1st	Ditto	96
Josiah Jones, 2d	Ditto	96
Seth Johnson	Ditto	64
Moses Knowland	Ditto	96
Abner Kent	Ditto	96
John Knowles	Ditto	32
Anmi Kelton	Ditto	24
Isaac Kelley	Ditto	48
Henry Keler	Ditto	96
Stephen Knowlton, or Knotten	Ditto	32
Edward Kelly	Ditto	48
Ephraim Lane	Lieutenant Colonel	20
Thomas Linnen	Corporal	32
William Lucas	Private	96
Crosby Luce	Gunner	48
Nathaniel Ladd	Private	48
William Leaver, alias Lavar	Ditto	48
Oliver P. Lewis	Ditto	96
John Lloyd	Ditto	96
James Lawler	Ditto	96

4

A—Continued.

Name	Rank	At $136 50 per annum.
Jonathan Lawrence	Ensign	136 50
John Levet	Private	72
John Lee	Ditto	96
Noah Luce	Ditto	64
James Lucus	Ditto	96
James Lamb	Ditto	72
Harvey Lawton	Ditto	32
Luther Lawton	Ditto	32
Beza Ludden	Corporal	32
Job Lawton	Private	72
Elihu Lestor	Ditto	96
Reuben Mitchell	Ditto	96
Neal M'Arthur	Ditto	96
Isaac M'Kenney	Ditto	64
Benjamin Moody	Ditto	64
Benjamin Mastick	Ditto	96
Alexander Murray	Ditto	48
Benjamin Merrill	Ditto	64
Tilley Mead	Ditto	24
Elisha Munsell	Ditto	48
John Maynard	Lieutenant	81 60

A—Continued.

Name	Rank	per annum.
		At $ 48
Samuel Mears, Jr.	Private	48
William Messerve	Sergeant	64
John Morey	Ditto	48
Andrew Marshall	Ditto	48
Joseph Manning	Ditto	48
Thomas M'Curda	Ditto	48
John Miller	Private	48
Benjamin Morton	Ditto	48
Martin Magner	Ditto	96
John Manning	Ditto	96
Samuel Morse	Ditto	64
Jonathan Morrison	Ditto	48
Martin M'Donald	Ditto	96
Christopher Newbitt	Ditto	96
John Nickloss	Ditto	16
Daniel Nutting	Ditto	38 40
Timothy Northam	Ditto	32
Joseph Noyes	Lieutenant	34
Bartlett Nash	Corporal	32
Elisha Nash	Private	96
Reuben Newton	Sergeant	72

A—Continued.

		per annum.
Deergoodfor Nango	Private	At $64
James Nourse	Ditto	48
Isaac Neal	Ditto	72
Robert B. Orr	Sergeant	72
Joshua O'Donnell	Private	64
John Paul	Sergeant	76 80
Joseph Patterson	Ditto	48
George Parker	Private	76 80
Solomon Parsons	Ditto	76 80
John Priest	Ditto	64
Nathan Putnam	Ditto	8
Ebenezer Perkins	Marine	96
William Parker	Private	48
Joseph Peabody	Ditto	32
Amos Pierson	Sergeant	19 20
Job Priest	Ensign	52
Thomas Pratt	Private	64
Jonathan Patch	Ditto	96
Stephen Pachard	Ditto	57 60
Michael Pendergrass	Ditto	96
Joseph Pinkham	Ditto	48

A—Continued.

Name	Rank	At $96 per annum.
David Pearson	Private	96
Ransford Peet	Sergeant	48
Joseph Roberts	Carpenter	96
Elisha Rice	Corporal	96
Abner Rose	Matross	96
Moses Ramsdall	Private	96
Benjamin Rider	Ditto	96
Euphas Reed	Ditto	96
Jeremiah Robbins	Ditto	64
Joseph Rumrill	Ditto	64
Ebenezer Rowe	Seaman	96
Oliver Russell	Corporal	48
Benjamin Randall	Private	96
John Rice	Corporal	72
John Reed	Private	96
Asa Robbins	Ditto	72
Oliver Randall	Corporal	96
Enock Robbins	Private	96
Samuel Robbins	Ditto	48
John Richmond	Ditto	64
Robert Reynolds	Ditto	48

A—Continued.

Name	Rank	At $24 per annum.
William Russell	Private	
John Slewman	Captain	300
Eli Stearns	Sergeant	96
Ezekiel Spalding	Ditto	38 40
Joseph Saunders	Corporal	96
Jonathan Stevens	Ditto	48
John Stoak	Private	96
Anthony Shoppe	Ditto	96
Jonas Shattuck	Ditto	96
Lenas Sturdivant	Ditto	96
Moses Smith	Ditto	96
Enock Stocker	Ditto	6⅔
Anthony Starbard	Ditto	64
William Syms	Ditto	60
Daniel Stearns	Ditto	57 60
Abraham Sawyer	Ditto	48
Amasa Scott	Ditto	24
Robert Smith	Ditto	6⅔
Sylvanus Snow	Ditto	32
Abner Snow	Ditto	72
Moses Sanderson	Ditto	6⅔

A.—Continued.

				At $64 per annum.
Peleg Smith	Private	. . . . . .	. . . . .	64
Nathaniel H. Shed	Ditto	. . . . . .	. . . . .	48
John Shattuck	Ditto	. . . . . .	. . . . .	96
Benoni Staples	Ditto	. . . . . .	. . . . .	72
John Shirley	Ditto	. . . . . .	. . . . .	76 80
Nathaniel H. Sanderson	Ditto	. . . . . .	. . . . .	204
David Sherman	Lieutenant	. . . . . .	. . . . .	96
Elijah D. Savage	Private	. . . . . .	. . . . .	64
Christopher Stover	Ditto	. . . . . .	. . . . .	48
Aaron Swan	Ditto	. . . . . .	. . . . .	19 20
Peleg Sisson	Ditto	. . . . . .	. . . . .	72
James T. Smith	Ditto	. . . . . .	. . . . .	96
Robert Sherman	Ditto	. . . . . .	. . . . .	32
Jacob Skiff	Ditto	. . . . . .	. . . . .	48
George W Stephens	Ditto	. . . . . .	. . . . .	96
Jonathan Taft	Ditto	. . . . . .	. . . . .	96
Israel Thomas	Ditto	. . . . . .	. . . . .	96
Noah Taylor	Ditto	. . . . . .	. . . . .	96
Ephraim Taylor	Ditto	. . . . . .	. . . . .	64
Charles Thrasher	Ditto	. . . . . .	. . . . .	
Peleg Tallman	Yeoman	. . . . . .	. . . . .	81 60

A.—Continued.

		At $96 per annum.
Philip Taber -	Private -	32
Eliphalet Taylor -	Ditto -	38 40
Josiah Temple -	Ditto -	64
Hezekiah Thorndike -	Ditto -	32
Zebediah Tweed -	Ditto -	72
Jonathan Taylor -	Ditto -	32
Thomas Templeton -	Ditto -	240
David S. Townsend -	Captain -	48
Samuel S. Thompson -	Private -	32
Ebenezer Tuttle -	Ditto -	96
Samuel Taylor -	Ditto -	48
David Trull -	Ditto -	32
Samuel Thing -	Ditto -	48
William Tracy -	Matross -	181 33⅓
George Ulmer -	Lieutenant -	48
John Union, 1st. -	Private -	180
Philip Ulmer -	Lieutenant -	96
John Union, 2d. -	Private -	96
Amariah Vose -	Sergeant -	32
David Vickery -	Private -	96
John Vandeford -	Ditto -	

A.—Continued.

Name	Rank		per annum.
Samuel Varney	Private	At £82	
Moses White	Captain	240	
James Warren	Lieutenant	136	
Joseph Whitemore	Ditto	136	
David Wood	Sergeant	76 80	
Elijah Williams	Corporal	96	
William Watts	Private	96	
Joshua Winn	Ditto	76 80	
Joseph Ware	Ditto	96	
Asa Ware	Ditto	96	
Josiah Wright	Ditto	76 80	
Elisha Ward	Ditto	64	
Samuel Woodbury	Marine	64	
Wareham Warner	Private	57 60	
Moses Wing	Drummer	96	
Samuel Warner	Private	48	
Samuel Willington	Ditto	48	
Nahum Wright	Sergeant	12	
William Warren	Lieutenant	102	
James Wesson	Colonel	300	
James Walsh	Matross	96	

5

A.—Continued.

Name	Rank			per annum. At $24
Dean Wyman	Private			At $24
Samuel Williams	Ditto			96
William Wyatt	Ditto			72
John Webb	Ditto			32
Charles Wait	Ditto			72
Luther Weatherly	Corporal			96
Daniel M. Wight	Sergeant			48
Dean Weymouth	Private			96
Andrew White	Sergeant			96
John Whalen	Private			96
Jeremiah Woodcock	Ditto			48
Cornelius Williams	Ditto			48
John Wyman	Ditto			72
Jesse Warner	Ditto			48
Adam Walker	Musician			72
Elias Ware	Private			48
Samuel Winn	Ditto			48
Theophilus Witherell	Ditto			72
Ehnathan Ward	Ditto			72
Simon Young	Ditto			48.

A.—Continued.

						per annum.
Nathaniel F. York	-	-	-	Private	-	At $24
John Young	-	-	-	Ditto	-	480
Philip Yeaton	-	-	-	Ditto	-	33

Making 418 for Massachusetts.

A.—Continued.

LIST *of Invalid Pensioners of the United States, belonging to the District of Maine, and paid at Portland, with the annual allowance annexed to each, viz:*

		per annum.
Elijah M. Barton	Sergeant - -	At $48
Asa Baker	Private -	64
Joseph Bryant	Second lieutenant	180
Ebenezer Bodwell	Corporal -	96
John Condon	Private '	24
David Cook	Captain -	200
Timothy Chadbourne	Sergeant	48
Daniel Carr	Private -	96
Samuel Emerson	Ditto -	48
Jeremiah Elwell	Ditto -	76 80
Jacob Frost	Ditto -	48
Abel Gossom	Ditto -	96
Asa Holt	Sergeant -	32
William Harris	Private -	48
Thomas House	Ditto -	32
Charles Hodgdon	Ditto -	48
Joel Ireland	Ditto -	38 40
John Lunt	Ditto -	96

A.—Continued.

			At $96 per annum.
Jedediah Lumbard	Private		$96
Nathaniel Martin	Ditto		48
Benjamin Marshall	Ditto		48
Isaac Osgood	Ditto		48
John Parker	Ditto		96
William Rideout	Ditto		96
Benjamin Roundy	Ditto		48
James Swett	Ditto		32
Noah Sinclair	Corporal		48
Nathaniel Strout	Private		72
Uriah Spearin	Ditto		24
William Trask	Ditto		96
Stephen Thomas	Corporal		32
Abraham Wellman	Ditto		96
Stephen Webster	Private		96
William White	Corporal		32
George Ward	Private		48
Thomas Webster	Sergeant		96

Making 36 for the District of Maine.

A —Continued.

List of Invalid Pensioners of the United States belonging to the state of Connecticut, and paid at Middletown, with the annual allowance to each annexed, viz:

		per annum.
Thomas Avery -	Lieutenant	At $204
Park Avery "	Ditto	96
Ebenezer Avery "	Corporal -	48
David Atkins "	Private -	96
Gad Asher "	Ditto	96
Abner Andruss -	Ditto	96
Daniel Avery "	Ditto	57 60
Amos Avery "	Ditto	48
Samuel Andrus -	Corporal -	72
Smith Ames "	Private -	96
Nathaniel Austin	Ditto	72
Daniel Bouten -	Captain -	180
Daniel Bushnell -	Private "	96
Simeon Bishop -	Ditto	96
William Burrows "	Ditto	96
Daniel Bill "	Ditto	96
Stephen Branum "	Ditto	96
Samuel Burdion "	Ditto	96
Benjamin Bennet "	Ditto	38 40
John Beardsly, Jr.	Ditto	96
Jedediah Brown	Ditto	32

A.—Continued.

		At $24 per annum.
Elisha Burrows	Private	24
Josiah Beaumont	Ditto	48
Walter Burdick	Ditto	48
Edward Bassett	Ditto	24
Robert Bailey	Ditto	64
David Blackman	Ditto	48
Aner Bradley	Sergeant	24
Oliver Bumham	Ditto	72
Isaac Buel	Private	96
Joseph Button	Ditto	64
Seth Boardman	Private	96
William C. Bebee	Ditto	156
Hezekiah Bailey	Ensign	48
Benjamin Brockway	Private	72
Paul Bebee	Ditto	96
Ephraim Brown	Sergeant	96
Orra Bradsley	Private	180
James Bnbridge	Captain	240
Willard Blanchard	Ditto	240
Ebenezer Coe	Ditto	70 40
Richard Chamberlain	Private	

A.—Continued.

Name	Rank	At $ per annum.
John Clark	Private	96
Mathew Cadwell	Ditto	96
Benoni Connell	Ditto	96
Jirah Carter	Ditto	96
Timothy Ceasar	Ditto	96
Benjamin Close	Ditto	76
Amaziah Chappell	Ditto	72
Elisha Clark	Ditto	48
Jonah Cook	Ditto	96
Henry Cone	Ditto	96
Simon Crosby	Ditto	64
Nathaniel Church	Ditto	48
William Clark	Ditto	72
John Clark, 2d.	Ditto	57 60
Horace Clark	Ditto	96
Jesse J. Clark	Ditto	24
Nathaniel Clark	Ditto	72
Jared Carter	Sergeant	96
Ebenezer Duran	Private	96
Lothrop Davis	Sergeant	96
Israel Dibble	Private	86

A.—Continued.

Name	Rank			At $96 per annum.
Gersham Dormon	Private			96
John Daboll	Ditto			12
Isaac Durand	Private			48
Francis David	Corporal			32
Amos Dewey	Private			48
Harmon Dewey	Ditto			48
Henry Dixon, or Dickson	Ditto			48
Stephen Everts	Ditto			96
William Edmonds	Ditto			64
Thomas Farnham	Sergeant			57 60
Bamford A Ferris	Private			96
Zachoeus Fargo	Ditto			48
Henry Kilmore	Ditto			48
Joel Fox	Ditto			48
Ami Fenn	Ditto			48
Andrew Griswold	Lieutenant			181 33⅓
Sherman Gardner	Private			96
Henry Gilner	Ditto			96
Andrew Gallup	Ditto			64
Luke Guyant	Ditto			96
Robert Gallup	Ditto			24

A.—Continued.

Name	Rank	At $48 per annum.
James Guthrie	Private	48
Joseph Hanup	Ditto	96
John Herron	Ditto	48
Nathan Hawley	Corporal	96
Daniel Hewitt	Sergeant	32
Benjamin Howd	Private	72
Elijah Hoyt	Ditto	24
David Hubble	Ditto	96
Nathani-l Hewitt	Ditto	72
David Hurd	Ditto	96
Zebina Hubbard	Ditto	72
Shubal P. Hibbard	Sergeant	96
Nathaniel Heaton	Corporal	96
Charles Jones	Private	96
Johiel Judd	Ditto	76 80
Lent Ives	Private	48
Caleb Jewitt	Ditto	32
William Johnson	Ditto	48
Jared Knapp	Sergeant	96
Lemuel King	Private	96
William Kingsbury	Sergeant	48

A.—Continued.

		At $96 per annum.
Peter Lewis	Private	At $96
Phineas Lake	Ditto	96
William Leach	Ditto	96
Christian Lathamp	Ditto	72
Naboth Lewis	Ditto	64
Samuel Lomis	Corporal	72
Nathaniel Lewis	Private	24
Elijah Lincoln	Ditto	96
Adam Larrabee	Captain	300
John Lynes	Private	72
Timothy Mix	Lieutenant	68
Andrew Mead	Ensign	104
Samuel Mitchell	Private	96
Samuel Mills, jun.	Ditto	48
John Morgan, 3d.	Ditto	64
Jacob Meach	Ditto	32
James Morgan, jun.	Ditto	48
Jeremiah Markham	Sergeant	96
Allyn Marsh	Corporal	48
Stephen Miner	Quarter gunner	48
Henry Magrath	Private	48

A.—Continued.

Name	Rank	per annum.
Jared Merrill	Corporal	At $32
John Miner	Private	96
Ransom Mix	Ditto	96
Stephen Mack	Ditto	64
Gardiner Morey	Ditto	96
Mark Noble	Ditto	96
Ephraim F. Nichols	Corporal	84
David Orcutt	Private	96
Joseph Otis	Ditto	48
William Owens	Ditto	96
Benjamin O'Cain	Ditto	48
Alexander Phelps	Ditto	96
David Pod	Ditto	96
Thomas Parmelie	Sergeant	12
Chandler Pardie	Private	84
Daniel Preston	Ditto	32
Enos Petott	Ditto	38 40
Aaron Peck	Ditto	64
Jesse Perkins	Ditto	64
John Rood	Ditto	76 80
Jeremiah Ryan	Ditto	96

A.—Continued.

		At $96 per annum.
Moses Reymond	Private	38 40
Oliver Rogers	Ditto	96
Solomon Reynolds	Ditto	96
Samuel Rosetter	Ditto	72
Elijah Royce	Ditto	48
Adonijah B. Rogers	Corporal	96
Amos Robinson	Private	48
Russell P. Rogers	Ditto	72
Clark Rood	Ditto	48
Anson Roye	Ditto	96
Aaron Roberts	Ditto	96
Josiah Smith	Ditto	96
Edward Stanton	Ditto	64
Josiah Strong	Ditto	64
John Starr	Ditto	48
Selah Scoffield	Ditto	240
William Seymour	Ditto	24
Benjamin Seely	Ditto	64
Elihu Sabin	Ditto	24
Thomas Shepherd	Ditto	96
Amos Skeee	Ditto	

A.—Continued.

Name	Rank	At $96 per annum.
Heber Smith	Sergeant	24
Aaron Smith	Private	48
Edmund Smith	Ditto	72
Samuel Stillman	Ditto	120
Aaron Stevens	Captain	76 80
Peter Smith	Private	76 80
John Smith	Ditto	72
Daniel Stanton	Ditto	24
Samuel H. Steel	Ditto	96
Abel Shoales	Ditto	64
John W. Smith	Ditto	57 60
William Tarball	Corporal	64
Aaron Tuttle	Private	96
Enoch Turner, jun.	Ditto	24
Levi Tuttle	Ditto	72
John Titus	Ditto	96
Isaiah Twitchell	Ditto	180
John A. Thomas	Captain	48
Samuel Woodcock	Sergeant	57 60
Constant Webb	Ditto	96
John Wakle	Private	

A.—Continued.

			per annum.
Joseph Waterman	Private	. . . .	At $64
Benjamin Weed, jun.	Ditto	. . . .	48
Thomas Williams	Ditto	. . . .	96
Jacob Williams	Ditto	. . . .	48
Richard Watrous	Ditto	. . . .	72
Seth Weed	Lieutenant	. . . .	81 60
James Wayland	Private	. . . .	32
Joseph Weeks	Ditto	. . . .	96
Samuel Whitemore	Ditto	. . . .	48
Jonah S. Wood	Ditto	. . . .	32
Hezekiah White	Ditto	. . . .	48

Making 200 Invalid Pensioners for Connecticut.

A.—Continued.

List of Invalid Pensioners of the United States, belonging to the state of Rhode Island, and paid at Providence, with the annual allowance to each annexed, viz:

		At $240	per annum.
Thomas Arnold .	Captain .	86 40	
Abijah Adams .	Private .	48	
John Armsbury .	Ditto .	67 20	
William Bastow .	Sergeant .	96	
Edward Bennet .	Private .	76 80	
Jacob Briggs .	Ditto .	96	
George Bradford .	Ditto .	360	
William Barton .	General .	96	
Ezra Chase .	Private .	67 20	
James Chappel .	Ditto.	57 60	
Levi Caesar .	Ditto .	32	
Rowland Chadsey .	Ditto .	4	
Jonathan Davenport .	Ditto .	96	
Comfort Eddy .	Ditto .	48	
John Elliot .	Ditto .	96	
Edward Gavett .	Ditto .	76 80	
Prince Green .	Ditto .	48	
Richard Hopkins .	Ditto .	48	
William Lunt .	Ditto .		

A.—Continued.

		per annum.
John Mowry	Private	At $43 20
Edward Peirce	Sergeant	96
Joseph A. Richards	Corporal	67 20
John Slocum	Private	96
Richard Sephton	Ditto	96
Charles Scott	Ditto	96
Benoni Simmons	Gunner	96
Nathaniel Sheldon	Sergeant	96
Zachariah Sailor	Artificer	32
Noel Tabor	Corporal	43 20
Benjamin Tompkins	Marine	96
Prince Vaughn	Private	0 40
Edward Vase	Sergeant	16
Guy Watson	Private	48

Making 31 Invalid Pensioners for Rhode Island.

7

A—Continued.

List of *Invalid Pensioners of the United States, belonging to the state of* Vermont, *and paid at* Bennington, *with the annual allowance to each annexed, viz:*

		per annum.
Welcome Ainsworth	Private	At $ 96
Lyman Allen	Ditto	32
Alanson Adams	Ditto	72
Jonathan Allen	Ditto	32
William Beden	Corporal	57 60
Samuel Bradish	Private	96
Daniel Brown	Ditto	96
Elijah Barnes	Ditto	24
Elijah Bennet	Ditto	48
Thomas Brush	Ditto	24
David Brydia	Ditto	48
Joseph Bird	Ditto	76 80
Alexander Barr	Ditto	24
Ezra Bellows	Ditto	96
John Bell	Ditto	48
Jonathan Bowers	Corporal	96
Freeman Blakely	Private	96
David Barber	Ditto	32

A—Continued.

Name	Rank				At $ per annum.
Joshua Buzel	Private	.	.	.	64
Reuben Butler	Ditto	.	.	.	32
Jos. H. Bryant	Ditto	.	.	.	32
Elial Bond	Sergeant	.	.	.	72
Daniel Boynton	Private	.	.	.	72
Daniel Bennet	Ditto	.	.	.	48
Stephen Barnard	Ditto	.	.	.	64
Ephraim Bowen	Ditto	.	.	.	24
Alfred Barrell	Sergeant	.	.	.	48
George Beck	Private	.	.	.	96
Benjamin Butcher	Ditto	.	.	.	72
James Campbell	Ditto	.	.	.	48
Edward Clark	Sergeant	.	.	.	24
Elisha Capron	Private	.	.	.	48
Silas Curtis	Ditto	.	.	.	48
Shubal Carpenter	Ditto	.	.	.	72
Solomon Clark	Ditto	.	.	.	24
Frederick Carter	Ditto	.	.	.	48
Levi Cary	Ditto	.	.	.	48
Jacob Chase	Ditto	.	.	.	48
Ezekiel Cook	Ditto	.	.	.	48

A.—Continued.

	Rank	per annum.
John W. Cushing	First lieutenant	At $204
Oliver Darling	Private	96
Calvin Dyke	Ditto	96
John Day	Artificer	48
Samuel Eyers	Private	96
Daniel Evans	Ditto	48
Jason Evans	Ditto	96
Edward Emmery	Sergeant	32
Richard Fairbrother	Private	96
Nathan Ford	Ditto	38 40
Frederick Fuller	Sergeant	96
Daniel French	Private	96
Joseph Fields	Ditto	32
Chester Fletcher	Ditto	48
Charles French	Sergeant	48
William Fisk	Private	64
Asa Gould	Ditto	96
Benjamin Gould	Ditto	48
Amasa Glover	Ditto	38 40
Ezra Gates	Ditto	64
Gideon Griggs	Ditto	48

A—Continued.

Name	Rank	per annum.
John M. Goodrch	Private	At $32
Bethuel Goodrich	Ditto	48
Solomon Gibbs	Ditto	24
Zera Green	Corporal	2½
Isaac Gleason	Private	48
Moses Glazier	Ditto	32
Joshua Greaves	Ditto	96
William Hazletine	Ditto	96
Jedediah Hyde	Captain	180
Zimri Hill	Private	48
Lewis Hurde	Sergeant	96
Jared Hinckley, jun.	Private	48
Jonas Hobart	Ditto	48
Martin Hatch	Corporal	24
Timothy B Henderson	Sergeant	96
William Humphrey	Corporal	32
Arteban Hoyt	Private	48
Eli Hynes, or Hynds	Ditto	64
Jonas Harrington	Corporal	96
Uriah Higgins	Private	96
John Hadley	Ditto	72

A.—Continued.

Name	Rank	At $32 per annum.
Nathan Jacques	Private	32
Seth Ingram	Sergeant	84
Henry Jones, 1st.	Private	48
William Jourdan	Musician	96
Henry Jones, 2d.	Sergeant	48
Elijah Knight	Private	96
William Kellogg	Ditto	72
Noadiah Kibbee	Ensign	104
George W. King	Private	48
Joseph B. Lovewell	Ditto	96
Jonathan Lake	Corporal	48
Jonathan Lyon	Private	96
Irving Lane	Ditto	24
Anson Lilly	Ditto	96
David Lathe	Ditto	48
Thomas Lowe	Ditto	96
Levi Lane	Ditto	72
Arza Lee	Ditto	96
Samuel Lynds	Ditto	96
Eleazer Martin	Ditto	64
Elenezer M'Ilvane	Ditto	96

A—Continued.

		At $64 per annum.
William Martin	Private	96
Richard Millen	Ditto	96
Abraham Merryfield	Ditto	96
John M'Cloud	Ditto	96
John Morgan	Ditto	96
Peter Mossey	Ditto	95
Miller Mosier	Ditto	96
John M'Coy	Corporal	96
Adam Muir	Private	72
John Newton	Sergeant	48
Nehemah Pierce	Private	96
Levi Plumberry	Ditto	64
Edward Putney	Ditto	96
Abraham Poor	Ditto	48
Justus Powers	Ditto	32
Elisha Reynolds	Ditto	64
Prince Robinson	Ditto	96
Lemuel Rich	Ditto	96
William Richards	Ditto	48
John Roberts	Corporal	32
Thomas B. Reed	Private	64

A—Continued.

Name	Rank	per annum.
Uriah Stone	Steward	At $96
Ephraim Smith	Private	96
Philo Stoddard	Ditto	6¼
James Stevens	Ditto	6¼
Reuben Stiles	Ditto	72
John Shattuck	Corporal	32
Isaac Spooner	Private	72
Alba Southard	Ditto	48
Calvin Stewart	Sergeant	32
Ebenezer Smith	Private	32
Thomas Torrance	Ditto	48
Benjamin Tower	Ditto	96
Annias Tubb	Ditto	48
John Talman	Ditto	96
Amasa Turner	Ditto	96
Church Tabour	Sergeant	72
Festus L. Thompson	Third Lieutenant	168
Samuel Thompson	Sergeant	72
Nathaniel Thompson	Private	48
Horace B Thompson	Ditto	72
Abel Woods	Ditto	96

A—Continued.

					per annum.
Aaron Wilder	. . . .	.	. .	Private	At $96
Jonathan Woolly	. .	. .	Ditto		96
Zibu Woodworth	.	.	Ditto		96
William Waterman	.	.	Ditto		32
John Wilson	.	.	Sergeant		32
Isaac Webster	.	.	Ditto		48
Samuel White	.	.	Ditto		72
Richard C. Wear	.	.	Private		96
Rexford Wittum	.	.	Ditto		48
John Williams	.	.	Ditto		72
David Warren	.	.	Ditto		48
Robert White	.	.	Ditto		480
Abraham Woodard	.	.	Ditto		96
Peter Wilhelm	.	.	Ditto		48
Joshua Wade	.	.	Ditto		96
Benjamin Weed	.	.	Ditto		72
Henry Wilson	.	.	Ditto		48

Making 161 Invalid Pensioners for Vermont.

8

A.—Continued.

LIST of *Invalid Pensioners of the United States, belonging to the State of New York, and paid at the city of New York, with the annual allowance annexed to each, viz:*

		At $96 per annum.
James Adams	Sergeant	96
Mathew Adams	Private	76 80
Garrett Abell	Ditto	57 60
Edward Armstrong	Ditto	57 60
Jacob Acker	Ditto	38 40
Richard Allison	Ditto	
Daniel Averill	Ditto	48
George Armstrong	Ditto	48
Edward Alberton	Ditto	96
Norman Anderson	Ditto	96
Philip Allen	Ditto	48
Earl Armstrong	Ditto	48
Abraham Asten	Ditto	96
Elisha Adams	Artificer	72
Ephraim J. Andrews	Private	48
Daniel Acker	Ditto	32
Oliver Andrews	Ditto	32
Silas Alexander	Ditto	64

A.—Continued.

		per annum.
		At $48
Isaac Ackerman	Private -	225
John T. Arrowsmith	Major -	225
John Adams	Sergeant -	48
Waterman Baldwin	Private -	96
Joshua Barnum	Captain -	240
Nathan Bradley	Private -	96
Henry Brewster	Lieutenant	136
David Brown	Ensign	124 80
Nicholas Barrett	Lieutenant	153
Thomas Buice	Ensign	124 80
James Burgess	Quartermaster sergeant	38 40
Silas Barber	Sergeant	96
Jonas Belknap	Ditto	32
Joshua Bishop	Matross	57 60
John Bennett	Private	96
John Butler	Ditto	96
Timothy Bowen	Ditto	96
Nicholas Bovie	Ditto	96
Edward Benton	Ditto	96
John Baxter	Ditto	76 80
John Brooks	Ditto	57 60

A.—Continued.

Name	Rank	At $57 60 per annum.
Obidiah Banks	Private	48
George H. Bell	Ditto	38 40
Michael Brooks	Ditto	38 40
Nicholas Brown	Ditto	38 40
Batus Bradenburgh	Ditto	96
Edward Bates	Ditto	48
Thomas Baldwin	Sergeant	72
Thomas Brooks	Private	48
Jedidiah Brown	Ditto	96
William Burritt	Ditto	204
Celeb Brewster	Lieutenant	24
Obedidiah Brown	Private	96
Henry Bouce	Ditto	96
Benjamin Benjamin	Ditto	76 80
James Beers	Ditto	96
Benjamin Bartlett	Sergeant	96
Aaron Brink	Private	96
John Bogge, alias, Bogue	Ditto	240
Selah Benton	Captain	64
Nehemiah W. Badger	Private	96
Levi Bishop	Ditto	

A.—Continued.

Name	Rank	At $240 per annum.
William Biggar	Captain	136
Frederick Brown	Lieutenant	72
James Bailey	Private	72
John Bennett	Ditto	72
Jonathan Bayley	Ditto	48
Ansel Beckwith	Ditto	153
James Boardman	First Lieutenant	240
Jesse Beach	Captain	96
John Belar	Private	48
David Butler	Corporal	48
James Brown	Private	72
Matthias Brown	Ditto	96
William Bennett	Ditto	32
Philander Benjamin	Ditto	48
Cavin Barnes	Ditto	96
Alpheus W. Briggs	Ditto	96
Joshua Box	Ditto	32
Edmund Barrett	Ditto	64
Henry Barnaby	Ditto	32
Reuben Baldwin	Sergeant	96
Philip Bovee	Private	96

A.—Continued.

Name	Rank	At $64 per annum.
Asahel Burgess	Private	
William C. Baker	Ditto	48
David Bartlett	Ditto	96
Jeremiah Bonner	Ditto	57 60
Charles Barber	Fifer	64
Thomas Broughton	Private	48
John Baird, alias, Bayard	Ditto	96
Charles Burbridge	Second Lieutenant	180
Bethuel Bump	Private	32
Edward Burt	Ditto	96
Jeptha Brown	Ditto	48
Samuel Benedict	Ditto	96
James Boyce	Ditto	96
Cornelius Blauvelt	Ditto	64
Edmund Badger	Sergeant	48
Gershom H. Brittin	Private	64
John Baxter, 2d.	Ditto	48
Peter Boyce	Ditto	48
Jotham Buzzell	Ditto	48
Joseph Bennett	Ditto	48
William Bundy	Ditto	48

A.—Continued.

		At $32 per annum.
Daniel Bennett, 1st.	Private	48
William Brown	Ditto	96
Benjamin Bailey	Ditto	72
Edward Burlison	Ditto	48
Jonathan Barney	Ditto	96
Jacob Baker	Artificer	96
Isaac Barker	Sergeant	48
Daniel Bennett, 2d.	Private	48
John Brownwell	Ditto	72
Jonathan Baker	Ditto	48
Hiram Buchanan	Ditto	82
Samuel Bowman	Ditto	48
David Bebels	Ditto	96
Peter Beam	Ditto	96
Charles T. Butler	Second Lieutenant	180
Peter Covenhoven	Sergeant	96
Thomas Carpenter	Lieutenant	108 80
Joseph Cutler	Ensign	156
Philo Carfield	Sergeant	38 40
Thomas Crawford	Bombadier	96
Edward Callaghan	Private	96

A.—Continued.

Name	Rank			per annum.
John Cooper	Private	.	.	At £96
Gershum Curvin	Ditto	.	.	96
Adam Coppernoll	Ditto	.	.	96
David Cady	Ditto	.	.	96
Daniel Culver	Ditto	.	.	96
Amos Camp	Ditto	.	.	64
Francis Courtney	Ditto	.	.	64
Gilbert Carrigan	Ditto	.	.	57 60
John Crum	Ditto	.	.	57 60
Phineas Coxe	Ditto	.	.	48
William Champermais	Ditto	.	.	72
Bussell Chappell	Ditto	.	.	48
Henry Challer	Ditto	.	.	96
Aaron Crane	Sergeant	.	.	48
Albert Chapman	Captain	.	.	120
John Cramer	Private	.	.	48
Peter Conyme	Adjutant	.	.	96
Ambrose Crane	Private	.	.	64
Dan Culver	Ditto	.	.	96
Daniel Cushmun	Corporal	.	.	76 80
James Crosslay	Private	.	.	48

A.—Continued.

			per annum.
Eli Capen	Private		At $72
Elijah Caleb	Ditto		64
William B. Cook	Ditto		48
Charles Cortivate	Ditto		96
Abner Case	Ditto		48
John W. Campbell	Sergeant		72
William Clark	Lieutenant		136
William Cooney	Private		96
John Cross	Corporal		48
James Colburn	Artificer		96
Henry Cramer	Private		48
Samuel Cannon	Ditto		96
John Campbell	Ditto		48
Stephen M. Gonger	Ditto		48
John Coons	Ditto		48
Moses Crissey	Ditto		96
John Conley	Ditto		32
John Conden	Ditto		96
Samuel Carl	Ditto		24
William G. Camp	Ensign		156
James Curran	Private		48

A—Continued

		At $48 per annum.
Theodore Clafflin	Corporal	96
James Carney	Private	32
Eastman Corbin	Ditto	96
George Cook	Ditto	96
John Cancannon	Ditto	48
Martin Carroll	Ditto	48
Levi H. Christian	Ditto	96
Thomas Crawford	Ditto	96
Nedabiah Cass	Ditto	64
Stephen Comings	Ditto	72
Patrick Griggins	Ditto	48
Robert Cockle	Ditto	48
Joseph Carpenter	Ditto	96
Leonard Curtis	Ditto	48
Amos Carr	Ditto	64
Samuel J. Chapman	Ditto	32
Daniel Christie	Ditto	48
Calvin Childs	Sergeant	72
Richard Clark	Private	96
David Corey	Ditto	48
William Carroll	Ditto	

A.—Continued.

		per annum.
Stephen Collins	Private	At $96
Leonard Chaffe	Ditto	32
Frederick Campbell	Ditto	32
Augustus Cleaveland	Captain	120
Jonathan D. Carrier	Private	48
Ezra Crane	Ditto	96
Archibald C. Crary	First Lieutenant	153
James Corbin	Private	96
Jotham Campbell	Corporal	72
James A. Chadwick	Ditto	32
Laban Cooper	Private	48
Paul Cassino	Ditto	48
Ebenezer Cole	Second lieutenant	180
Charles W. Collins	Private	96
Michael Cunningham	Ditto	48
Charles P. Christian	Sergeant	64
Adam Coward	Corporal	48
Orvin C. Cadwell	Ditto	96
Ithamer Cooley	Private	96
Caleb Crane	Second lieutenant	90
John Cronk	Private	48

A—Continued.

Name	Rank	At $47 per annum.
Elias G. Crego	Private	
Barnard Curry	Corporal	96
Hackalia Doolittle	Private	48
Hansmark Demoth	Captain	240
Francis Delong	Lieutenant	68
Andrew Dunlap	Sergeant	96
Thomas Duncan	Ditto	96
William Drew	Corporal	57 60
Nathan Davis	Private	96
James Dunlap	Ditto	96
Matthias Decamp	Ditto	96
George Dunkill	Ditto	96
Samuel Decker	Ditto	96
Marshall Dixon	Ditto	38
Thomas Done	Matross	96
James Dole	Second lieutenant	120
Peter Demarest	Private	96
John De Voe	Ditto	96
Benjamin Denslow	Ditto	96
Gerardus Dingham	Ditto	96
Jared Duncan	Ditto	96

A.—Continued.

Name	Rank	At $48 per annum.
William Doty	Private	72
Stephen Dodge	Ditto	64
Seth Davis	Ditto	72
Joseph Decker	Corporal	48
Daniel Dve	Private	72
Erastus Desbrow	Ditto	48
John Doty	Ditto	72
James Durney	Ditto	96
John C. Boss	Sergeant	32
John Dabzell	Private	96
Edward Duffy	Ditto	180
John P. Dieterich	Second lieutenant	24
John Delonge	Private	48
Justin Dickinson	Ditto	48
Ishmael Davis	Ditto	76 80
Thomas Durland	Ditto	96
John Depew	Corporal	152
Thomas Darling	First lieutenant	180
Henry De Witt	Second lieutenant	76 80
Isaac Elwood	Corporal	96
Nathan Ellis	Private	

A.—Continued.

		per annum.
William Elberton	Private	At $ 96
Jeremiah Everitt	Ditto	48
Peter Eager	Ditto	96
Alfred Eldridge	Ditto	48
Oliver Emmerson	Corporal	72
Joshua Edwards	Private	64
Orrigen Eaton	Ditto	96
Mathias Emerick	Ditto	72
Joseph Emmonds	Ditto	48
David Ervin	Ditto	96
Peter Eaton	Ditto	96
Isaac Evans	Ditto	96
Nathaniel Enos	Ditto	57 60
John Erwin, (or Irwin)	Ditto	96
Thomas Evans	Ditto	64
Samuel Elliott	Sergeant	32
John Frey	Brigade Major	300
Christian W. Fox	Captain	240
William Falkner	D to	90
Hackaliah Foster	Sergeant	48
Robert Feeks	Corporal	76 80

A—Continued.

Name	Rank		per annum.
Squire Fancher	Private	.	At $96
William Fogan	Ditto	.	96
Dancan Frazier	Ditto	.	96
John Foster	Ditto	.	96
Andrew Frank	Ditto	.	96
John Jost Foltz	Ditto	.	96
Jonathan Finch	Ditto	.	76 80
George Finckley	Ditto	.	76 80
Sylvanus Ferris	Ditto	.	57 60
Elisha Frizzle	Ditto	.	96
William Fancher	Ditto	.	38 40
John Ferris	Ditto	.	38 40
Elisha Farnham	Ditto	.	48
Elisha Forbes	Ditto	.	57 60
William Foster	Ditto	.	96
Elisha Fanning	Sergeant Major	.	48
Thomas Fitzgerald	Corporal	.	48
Nicholas Ford	Private	.	96
Herman Fisher	Sergeant	.	96
Eliphalet Filmore	Private	.	96
Joseph Foster	Ditto	.	96

A—Continued.

Name	Rank	At £96 per annum.
John B Fuller	Private	96
George Fitzsimmons	Ditto	48
Levi Frisbie	Ditto	96
Samuel Foster	Ditto	6¾
Timothy Ford	Ditto	48
Owen D. Farley	Ditto	96
Samuel Freeman	Ditto	96
Thomas Flood	Ditto	96
William Ferguson	Ditto	48
Timothy Fisher	Ditto	96
Ambrose Fuller	Ditto	32
George Fenton	Musician	48
Aran Fitzgerald	Private	72
William Farrington	Ditto	96
Donald Frazer	Major	300
John Furman	Private	96
Jabez Fisk	Ditto	48
Alexander Frazier	Musician	6¾
Jehiel Felt	Captain	160
Abel Follet	Private	64
Locklin Farry	Ditto	64

A.—Continued.

Name	Rank	At $ 96 per annum.
John Ferguson	Private	204
John L. Fink	First Lieutenant	24
Henry B. Ferris	Sergeant	64
William Fulkerson	Drummer	120
Edmund Foster	Captain	72
Joshua Foss	Private	78
Richard Garrison	Quarter Master	120
Jacob Gardider	Captain	181 33⅓
Nathaniel Gove	Lieutenant	181 3⅓
Samuel Gibbs	Ditto	57 60
Zachariah Green	Corporal	96
John Garnet	Private	96
Samuel Gardiner	Ditto	38 40
Benajah Geer	Ditto	24
Allen Gilbet	Ditto	48
Isaac Genung	Ditto	96
Burr Gilbert	Ditto	48
Simeon Gibbs	Corporal	48
John Gilbert	Sergeant	96
James Gorman	Matross	204
John Gifford	First Lieutenant	64
Samuel Gray	Private	64

10

A.—Continued.

Name	Rank	At $48 per annum.
Daniel Guthrie	Private	48
Joseph Gillet	Lieutenant	204
Pierre Griffin	Private	64
William O. Glass	Ditto	96
Daniel Gardiner	Ditto	72
Asa Glazier	Ditto	48
Samuel Gurnee	Ditto	96
George Gooding	Ditto	48
Charles Goodsell	Ditto	48
Rufus Green	Ditto	48
Samuel Grey	Ditto	72
Nathan Gates	Ditto	57 60
Peter Goodrick	Ditto	96
Jacob Groves	Ditto	48
Avery Griswold	Corporal	72
Gardner Goodspeed	Private	32
Moses George	Ditto	48
Allen Green	Ditto	64
Patrick Grennon	Sergeant	48
Thomas Hustler	Ditto	96
David Hall, Jr.	Ditto	96

A.—Continued.

		At $176 80 per annum.
George Helmar	Lieutenant	189
Mordicai Hall	Surgeon's Mate	96
Staats Hammond	Sergeant	38 40
John Hilton	Ditto	76 80
Stephen Hurlbret	Drummer	96
John Hink	Private	96
Joseph Harris	Ditto	88 20
Adam Hartman	Ditto	76 80
George Hansell	Ditto	64
Peter Hagaboom	Ditto	48
Thomas Hill	Ditto	38 40
Asa Hill	Ditto	24
Joseph Hager	Ditto	19 20
Henry Hopper	Ditto	19 20
John Hess	Lieutenant	90 66⅔
Barlet Hinds	Private	57 60
John Hubbard	Ditto	24
Humphrey Hunt		200 "Law, 23d Jan. 1805."
Charlotte Hazen	Captain	120
Joseph Harker	Sergeant	48
Peter Harford		

A.—Continued.

		$ per annum.
David Hamilton	Private	A $ 96
William Hedger	Ditto	96
William Hamma	Ditto	24
David Hawkins	Ditto	96
George Howard	Captain	240
John Hisrott	Private	48
John Huie	Captain	240
Zenas Hastings	Private	96
Charles Hagin	Ditto	96
Daniel Hannah	Ditto	48
Jeptha Hoar	Ditto	32
Caleb Hayward	Ditto	48
John Higgins	Ditto	48
Joseph Golmes	Sergeant	57 60
James Harvey	Private	24
Joel Hancock	Ditto	48
Lewis Hayat	Ditto	72
Moses Harrington	Ditto	96
Jarius Haskell	Ditto	64
Thomas Higgins	Ditto	48
Daniel Hammond	Corporal	96

A.—Continued.

Name	Rank	At $72 per annum.
John Herrick	Private	76 40
Waterman Harris	Ditto	64
Samuel Hays	Ditto	48
William J. Hendershott	Ditto	102
Arunah Hibbard	First lieutenant	48
Apollas Holcomb	Corporal	48
Hezekiah Hubbard	Private	96
Alpheus Hill	Ditto	96
William Hamma	Ditto	32
Samuel Haviland	Ditto	72
Joseph Hopkins	Sergeant	96
Nathaniel Harris	Private	48
Moses Head	Ditto	72
Aaron Haskins	Sergeant	72
Moses Hitchcock	Private	72
Abraham Hasbrouck	Ditto	96
James Horrica	Corporal	96
Samuel Jones	Sergeant	96
James Ivory	Private	38 40
William Jump	Ditto	38 40
William James	Ditto	

A.—Continued.

		At $120 per annum.
Elijah Janes	Lieutenant	120
John Johnson	Private	96
Thomas Judd	Ditto	72
Solomon Jenkins	Ditto	96
Abraham Johnson	Ditto	64
Ebenezer Jayne	Ditto	96
David Jenkins	Ditto	64
Justus Ingersoll	First Lieutenant	102
Samuel Jenner	Private	32
Jones Jones	Ditto	64
Harvey Johnson	Ditto	24
Jacob Innis, or Annis	Ditto	48
Ransom Isbel	Sergeant	32
Bennet Joy	Private	96
Samuel Jones	Ditto	48
Lewis Janes	Ditto	48
Severinus Koch	Sergeant	96
Johannes Koch	Ditto	57 60
Reuben King	Private	96
Joseph Knapp	Ditto	76 80
George Knox	Ditto	57 60

A.—Continued.

		At $57 60 per annum.
John Ketchum	Private	64
Abiel Knapp	Ditto	72
John King	Ditto	48
Elijah Knapp	Sergeant	96
Stephen Kellogg	Private	64
William Kelly	Ditto	48
Thomas Kierens	Ditto	64
Henry Kennedy	Sergeant	96
Barney Kelly	Private	48
Joseph Kerr	Ditto	64
Josiah Kean	Musician	64
Abial Kinsley	Private	72
John D. King	Ditto	48
Frederick Kortz	Sergeant	120
Nathaniel F. Knapp	Captain	48
Jacob Keyser	Private	64
Jeremiah Kimball	Sergeant	120
Elisha Kellogg	Captain	48
Eleazer Kellogg	Sergeant	48
John Kelly	Private	48
Tilley King	Ditto	64

80

A.—Continued.

			per annum.
James Korts	Sergeant		At $48
Victor Killen	Private -		72
David Kinniston	Corporal		64
Peter Kennedy	Private .		72
Thomas Lyon	Lieutenant		136
Henry Lewis	Ensign -		39
Robert Lang	Sergeant		76 80
Moses Lockwood	Gunner		57 60
William Lewis	Private		57 60
Michael Lyons	Ditto		76 80
Peter Lampman	Ditto		76 80
William Laken	Ditto		64
John Little	Captain		240
Thomas Lavis	Private		96
Ebenezer Lane	Ditto		96
Andrew Lawson	Ditto		96
William C. Lilly	Ditto		72
Merrill Lewis	Sergeant -		82
Uriah Limbocker	Private		96
William Loveborough	Ditto		24
Nathan Lockwood	Ditto		48

A.—Continued.

		per annum.
Robert Lockridge	Private	At $48
John J. Lord	Ditto	96
Abraham Lampman	Ditto	48
John Lassaw	Ditto	96
Wheeler Lamphier	Ditto	72
William Lingo	Ditto	48
Dudley Lamb	Second lieutenant	90
William Lippencott	Private	72
John Lovett	Major and aid-de-camp	300
Robert Lyon	Private	48
Joseph Livingston	Ditto	96
Israel Lawrence	Ditto	96
Thomas Laird	Ditto	48
Stephen Lush, jun.	Judge advocate & acting aid-de-camp }	300
Amon Lawrence	Private	96
Elijah Laton	Ditto	96
Henry Lake	Ditto	96
Aaron Longstreet	Ditto	96
James W. Lent, jun.	Ensign	156
Joseph M'Cracken	Major	300

A.—Continued.

			At $240	per annum.
John M'Kinstrey	Captain			
Michael Myers	Sergeant		96	
Lilleus Mead	Ditto		96	
Alexander M'Nish	Ditto		83 20	
Amos Miner	Ditto		48	
Mead Marshall	Gunner		96	
Alexander M'Coy	Bombadier		38 40	
George Mour	Private		96	
Charles M'Kenny	Ditto		96	
Gerardus Mook	Ditto		96	
John M'Intosh	Ditto		96	
Paul M'Fall	Ditto		76 80	
John Mosher	Ditto		76 80	
Samuel M'Kean	Ditto		57 60	
William Martine	Ditto		57 60	
Philip Martine	Ditto		57 60	
John Miller	Ditto		48	
Henry Murphy	Ditto		38 40	
Daniel Morvies	Ditto		38 40	
Hugh M'Master	Ditto		19 20	
Samuel Miller	Ditto		96	

A—Continued.

Name	Rank	per annum.
		At $96
Michael Malony	Private	240
Thomas Matchin	Captain	38 40
Joseph Mack	Private	48
Thomas M'Grath	Ditto	48
William M'Laland	Ditto	48
Donald M'Donald	Hostler	48
Michael M'Gowan	Private	64
Michael Magher	Ditto	180
Mordecai Myers	Captain	96
Spencer Mitchell	Private	96
Moses M'Keel	Ditto	32
Thomas Moore	Ditto	64
Benjamin M'Cleary	Ditto	72
Francis M'Donough	Ditto	64
James M'Minn	Ditto	72
Robert Marshall	Ditto	96
William M'Farland	Corporal	48
William Moore	Private	96
Noble Morse	Ditto	96
David M'Cracken, jun.	Ditto	96
John M'Nulty	Ditto	

A.—Continued.

			per annum. At $96
Patrick Mooney	Private		96
Chauncey Minor	Ditto		48
William Mitchell	Sergeant		96
Hugh Moore	Ditto		48
Harvey Moore	Ditto		32
John M'Laughlin	Ditto		96
Philip M'Cready	Ditto		96
Johannes Mullen	Ditto		96
Lewis Middleton	Ditto		48
Lewis Myers	Ditto		24
Clark Munger	Sergeant		32
John G. Munn	Second lieutenant		180
Abel Moore	Private		48
John Miller, 2d.	Ditto		96
Joseph Mitchell	Ditto		32
Aaron Matthews	Ditto.		96
Joseph M'Laughlin	Ditto		48
James M'Kean	Captain		300
Patrick M'Keon	Second lieutenant		180
William Moore	Sergeant		72
Francis Mosso	Private		64

A.—Continued.

		$ At per annum
John M'Coy	Private	48
Richard Moore	Ditto	48
Alfred Meade	Ditto	84
John Moor	Ditto	64
James Mullen	Ditto	32
Joshua Merrill	Ditto	48
Edward M'Gonigel	Sergeant	48
Noah Mitchell	Private	48
William M'Cullock	Ditto	32
Peter Mills	Captain	240
Louis Messellier	Second Lieutenant	180
Patrick M'Gowan, or M'Gown	Private	64
James Mears	Sergeant	96
Abraham Nealy	Lieutenant	136
Jacob Newkirk	Private	57 60
David Nicholls	Corporal	76 80
John Norcross	Private	38 40
Thomas Newins	Ditto	48
George Newton	Ditto	32
Nathan Nelson, jr.	Ditto	48
Seba Norton	Ditto	96
Thomas Newell	Ditto	96

A.—Continued.

		per annum.
Jeremiah Nichols	Private	At $32
Garret Oblenis	Ditto	48
Dennis Owens	Ditto	96
William Oahle	Ditto	96
John Oatman	Ditto	48
Bernard O'Conner	Second Lieutenant	180
Phelix O'Conner	Private	48
A. W. Odell	Captain	120
James Phillips	Private	48
Joseph Prenhop	Lieutenant	90 66⅔
Solomon Purdy	Sergeant	96
Joseph Pasmore	Ditto	96
Jonathan Purdy	Corporal	96
Thomas Powell	Private	96
Daniel Provost	Ditto	96
Stephen Plumb	Ditto	57 60
Silas Parish	Ditto	57 60
Adolph Pichard	D tto	48
Garret Peck	Ditto	38 40
Jared Palmer	Sergeant	48
Stephen Powell	Private	6

A.—Continued.

		per annum.
Joel Phelps	Private	At $48
Abner Prier	Ditto	48
Jonathan Pollard	Ditto	96
William Patterson	Ditto	96
Elisha Prior	Ditto	72
David Pendleton	Ditto	96
John Philips, 1st.	Corporal	76 80
James Pierce	Sergeant	96
John Philips, 2d.	Ditto	48
James Pollock	Private	48
Philip Philips	Ditto	48
Elisha Payne	Ditto	48
Loring Pottle	Ditto	96
Calvin P Perry	Corporal	96
Loring Palmer	First Lieutenant	204
William Pecure	Private	24
Samuel Palmer	Ditto	96
Henry Parks	Ditto	96
Josiah B. Pachard	Ditto	96
John Patterson	Ditto	96
Elisha Plumb	Ditto	24

A—Continued.

Name	Rank	per annum.
Reuben Patrick -	Private -	At $48
Robert Page	Ditto	72
David Price	Ditto	32
Daniel Palmer	Ditto	72
Evan Phillips	Ditto	32
Philo Porter	Sergeant	64
Samuel S. Page	Private	96
Joshua Penny	Quarter Master in the Navy	72
Charles Peabody	Private	96
Augustus Powers	Sergeant	64
William Platto	Private	96
John Provoe	Ditto	64
Jacob Piercy	Ditto	64
Abraham Per Lee	First Lieutenant -	136
William Perry	Private	96
Isaac Piercy	Second Lieutenant	180
John Quick	Private -	88 40
Timothy Quirk	Ditto	48
Nicholas Ritcher	Captain	240
John Requa	Private -	96
Israel Reeves	Ditto	96

A.—Continued.

Name	Rank	At $96 per annum.
Robert Robertson	Private	96
Jacob Rattenauer	Ditto	76 80
John Rice	Ditto	67 20
Joseph Rehern	Ditto	67 20
Hendrick Ritchmyer	Ditto	64
William Reymolds	Ditto	38 40
Frederick Rasberg	Ditto	19 20
John Renan	Ditto	48
Isaac Richards	Ditto	48
John Rogers	Ditto	57 60
James Reeves	Ditto	38 40
Benjamin Reynolds	Ditto	48
John B. Randall	Ditto	96
John R. Rappleye	Ditto	48
Isaiah Robison	Ditto	96
William Ray	Ditto	64
Henry Rynehart	Ditto	64
Eli Roe	Ditto	72
William Rand	Ditto	19 20
William Roberts, 1st.	Ditto	96
Peter Royer	Ditto	

12

A.—Continued.

Name	Rank	At $96 per annum.
Oliver Robbins	Private	48
John Russell	Ditto	96
Peter Rose	Ditto	48
William Roberts, 2d	Ditto	96
James Robinson	Ditto	48
Daniel Reed	Sergeant	96
Nicholas Rhodes	Private	96
Jesse Rumsey	Ditto	32
Alvin Richards	Quartermaster sergeant	24
Thomas Reed	Private	96
William Rogers	Ditto	96
Nicholas Rouce	Ditto	24
Michael Rider	Ditto	96
M. D. L. F. Bogers	Sergeant	96
Daniel Reaveau, or Reveau	Private	240
James J. Ryan	Captain	300
Tunis Riker	Major	240
Aiten Reynolds	Captain	48
John Richardson	Corporal	160
Thomas Robinson	Cornet	48
William Raymond	Private	

A—Continued.

				per annum.
Charles Rice	Private	. . . .	. . . .	At $48
Dedrick Royter	Ditto	. . . .	. . . .	32
Stephen Ring	Ditto	. . . .	. . . .	96
Conrad Root	Ditto	. . . .	. . . .	96
John St. John	Ditto	. . . .	. . . .	96
Samuel Shaw	Lieutenant	. . . .	. . . .	108 80
William Scott	Major	. . . .	. . . .	300
Philip Staats	Lieutenant	. . . .	. . . .	108 80
Josiah Smith	Ditto	. . . .	. . . .	136
James Stilwell	Sergeant	. . . .	. . . .	96
William Sloan	Ditto	. . . .	. . . .	64
John Stewart	Corporal	. . . .	. . . .	76 80
Daniel Stephens	Private	. . . .	. . . .	96
Pearl Sharks	Ditto	. . . .	. . . .	96
Robert Saunders	Ditto	. . . .	. . . .	96
John Shutliff	Ditto	. . . .	. . . .	96
Sylvanus Seely	Ditto	. . . .	. . . .	76 80
Cornelius Swartout	Ditto	. . . .	. . . .	76 80
James Scott, 1st.	Ditto	. . . .	. . . .	76 80
Henry Seber	Ditto	. . . .	. . . .	76 80
Abiel Sherman	Ditto	. . . .	. . . .	57 60

A—Continued.

Name	Rank	At $96 per annum.
Benjamin Smith	Private	57 60
James Smith	Ditto	57 60
George Stansel	Ditto	57 60
Garret Sulback	Ditto	57 60
Adam Stroback	Ditto	57 60
Edward Scot	Ditto	57 60
James Slater	Ditto	48
Thaddeus Seely	Ditto	48
Hans J st Snell	Ditto	88 40
George Schell	Ditto	96
Firley Stewart	Batteauman	72
Godfrey Sweet	Private	96
Sohn Sharp	Ditto	57 60
Eliphalet Sherwood	Ditto	48
Benjamin Sturges	Ditto	76 40
Edward Shell	Ditto	96
Job Snell	Ditto	24
Thomas P Smith	Ditto	96
Zachariah Sherwood	Ditto	48
John Sweeny	Lieutenant	102
John Sacket	Regiment Surgeon's Mate	270

A—Continued.

Name	Rank	At $8 32 per annum.
Joseph Swartwood	Private	48
John Shap	Ditto	72
John Smart	Ditto	96
Solomon Sanford	Ditto	72
Thaddeus Stocker	Ditto	72
Henry Sperry	Ditto	96
Ptolemy Sheldon	Ditto	96
Socrates Swift	Ditto	96
Samuel Schoonover	Ditto	64
Leverett Seward	Sergeant	76 80
Samuel Scott	Private	24
George St. Clair	Ditto	96
John Schofield	Ditto	96
Roswell Stephens	Ditto	96
Cadwallader L. Smith	Ditto	96
Peter W. Short	Musician	32
Thomas Smith	Private	48
James Stanton	Ditto	2
Thomas Sturtivant	Sergeant	96
Jonathan Smith	Private	64
Joseph Siscoe	Ditto	24

A—Continued.

Name	Rank	At $240 / per annum.
Thomas Sherwood	Captain	At $240
John Silsbe	Captain	180
William Shaft	Corporal	96
Nathaniel Stephens	Private	72
Benjamin Sweet	Ditto	24
Sala Sanford	Sergeant	48
Aaron Stafford	Adjutant	63 96
Frederick P. Stephenson	Lieutenant	96
Robert Shaw	First Lieutenant	204
Peter Simson, or Simpson	Private	96
Orange W. Strong	Ditto	24
John Spitzer	Ditto	48
James M. Scott	Ditto	96
David Stoddard	Ditto	96
John L. Shear	Ditto	48
Patrick Short	Ditto	48
Jacob Skates	Ditto	48
Asa C Stewart	Ditto	48
John N. Smith	Ditto	96
Thomas Smith	Drum Major	32
Isaac Sherman	Private	96

A.—Continued.

Name	Rank	At $64 per annum.
Benjamin Skinner	Private	64
Baxter Sharmon	Ditto	72
John Stoddard	Ditto	120
John B. Strong	Lieutenant and Adjutant	300
Silas Talbot	Lieutenant Colonel	181 33
Jacob Traviss	Lieutenant	96
John Thomas	Private	76 80
Ezekiel Travis	Ditto	76 80
Ebenezer Tyler	Ditto	64
Daniel Townsend	Ditto	51 20
William Tanner	Ditto	48
Asa Taylor	Ditto	57 60
John Taylor	Ditto	38 40
Alexander Tilford	Captain	180
Henry Ten Eyck	Marine	96
Abel Turney	Private	76 80
Daniel Treadwell	Sergeant	32
Robert Thompson	First lieutenant	153
Samuel Tappan	Private	72
John Thompson	Private	96
Erastus Taylor	Ditto	

A.—Continued.

Name	Rank	At $96 per annum.
Samuel Truby	Private	At $96
Caleb Torry	Ditto	48
Samuel Tubbs	Sergeant	48
Daniel Tibbits	Corporal	72
Mason Turner	Sergeant	96
James Tice	Private	64
Clark Tinker	Ditto	48
Henry Turner	Ditto	63 96
Ezekiel A. Turner	Sergeant	48
Selah Taylor	Private	48
William Thayer, jr.	Ditto	57 60
Benjamin Taylor	Ditto	72
John Ulters	Ditto	96
Henry C. Van Ransalier	Lieutenant Colonel	360
William Van Ward	Private	57 60
John Vaughn	Sergeant	24
Asa Vergill	Private	24
John Venus	Ditto	48
Isaac Vincent	Ditto	96
John Vanderbeck	Ditto	96
Abraham Vandenburg	Ditto	64

A.—Continued.

		At $96 per annum.
Joseph S. Van Driesen	Private	96
Abraham Valentine	Ditto	48
John J. Van Valkenburgh	Ditto	72
Daniel Vanderbogart	Ditto	64
Garret VanFleet, alias Vanvliet	Ditto	48
James L. Vinson	Sergeant	96
Samuel Van Schaack	Private	96
Martin Vanderworker	Ditto	72
Matthias Vanhorn	Ditto	96
James Vcohies	Sergeant	48
Ezekiel Varney	Private	48
Peter Van Beuren	Corporal	48
William Wallace	Lieutenant	108 80
James Wier	Corporal	83 20
David Wendall	Private	96
Thomas Ward	Ditto	96
George Waggoner	Ditto	96
Jacob Wright	Ditto	90
Thomas Wilson	Ditto	96
Abraham Wothlever	Ditto	96
David Wilson	Ditto	76 80

13

A.—Continued.

Name	Rank	At $76 80 per annum.
John Winn	Private	57 60
Lemuel Wood	Ditto	57 69
Nicholas Wabrath	Ditto	64
William White	Ditto	48
James Wills	Ditto	38 40
Ichabod Williams	Ditto	38 40
Isaiah Wright	Ditto	96
David Weaver	Ditto	96
Rozace Woodworth	Ditto	24
Ezekiel Williams	Ditto	24
George Walter	Corporal	96
Thomas Ward	Cadet	96
Mathew N. Whyte	Private	48
John Walch	Ditto	64
Herly Ward	Ditto	48
Bartholomew Walsh	Ditto	48
William Whittey	Ditto	96
George T. Wager	Ditto	72
Truman White	Ditto	96
Jacob Wright	Ditto	72
John B. Williams	Ditto	

A —Continued

		At $80 ¼ per annum.
Joseph Westcott.	Private	96
Peter Wyght	Sergeant	96
William Winch	Private	48
Corad Wager	Ditto	72
Richard Waldron	Artificer	96
John B. Williams	Private	48
Alexander Wilson	Ditto	72
Jonathan Wells	Ditto	96
Jeremiah H. Winney	Ditto	64
Jeremiah Woodman	Ditto	48
Elijah Woolworth	Ditto	48
William D. Wooster	Sergeant	48
George Wilson	Private	96
George Willsey	Ditto	96
George Weaver	Ditto	48
Charles West	Second lieutenant	180
John Wentworth	Private	96
John C. Wilford	Sergeant	48
Robert White	Private	48
John Williams	Second lieutenant	90
Nicholas Welch	Private	300

A.—Continued.

Name	Rank	per annum. At $48
Uriah Warren	Corporal	96
James Ward	Private	48
Dewitt Westlin	Ditto	96
Joseph Williams	Ditto	32
Darius Wadkins	Sergeant	96
Alexander Wilson	Private	96
Samuel White	Ditto	64
William Wood	Sergeant	96
Thomas Williams	Private	48
James Worrell	Ditto	96
Israel Waters	Matross	48
Joseph Willett	Private	96
John Ward	Ditto	72
James D. Wadsworth	Major	225
Oliver Wright	Private	48
John Wood	Ditto	96
John Yeunglove	Major	72
Gotfield Young	Corporal	96
John Yorden	Private	48
Nicholas Yorden	Ditto	19 20
Daniel Young	Ditto	67 20

A.—Continued

		At $96	per annum
Jesse Young	Private		
William Young	Ditto	96	
Abraham Yelverton	Ditto	96	
Nathan Young	Corporal	96	

Making 905 for New York

A.—Continued.

LIST of Invalid Pensioners of the United States, belonging to the State of New Jersey, and paid at Trenton, N. J. with the annual allowance to each annexed, viz:

Name	Rank	per annum.
Isaac Bennett	Sergeant	At $64
Barnes Bunn	Private	38 40
Benjamin Bishop	Ditto	38 40
James Boden	Ditto	48
John Brant	Ditto	48
Thomas Carhart	Corporal	96
Robert Coddington	Private	96
George Compton	Corporal	48
Randolph Clarkson	Private	48
Joseph Crill	Ditto	64
Merris Decamp	Sergeant	76 80
Daniel Dodd	Private	48
Jacob Dollas	Ditto	48
John Fergus	Ditto	38 40
Mahton Ford	Captain	240
John Fenton	Private	48
Daniel Guard	Ditto	48
Godfrey Garhart	Ditto	64

A.—Continued.

Name	Rank	At $93 60 per annum.
John Hampton	Ensign	At $93 60
Theophilus Hathaway	Private	96
Jacob Hall	Ditto	64
William Howell	Ditto	51 20
Benoni Hathaway	Captain	120
Nicholas Hoff	Private	96
James Heard	Lieutenant	102
James Jerolman	Ditto	27 20
Francis Jeffers	Private	33 40
William Johnson	Ditto	48
Samuel Kirkendake	Captain	120
Christian Khunn	Private	96
Aaron King	Ditto	64
Samuel Lindsley	Ditto	72
Samuel Leonard	Ditto	48
John Lashels	Corporal	96
John M'Clure	Private	96
Daniel Moffett	Ditto	48
Peter Neifes	Sergeant	76 80
Jabez Pembleton	Private	48
Silas Parrot	Lieutenant	81 60

A.—Continued.

			per annum.
Thomas Phillips	Private		At $348
Caleb Putney	Sergeant		72
Zachariah Pack	Ditto		96
John Quinby	Private		56 20
Andrew Ross	Ditto		25 60
Jacob Rider	Ditto		96
Jonathan Snowden	Lieutenant		20½
Daniel Snalbaker	Private		96
James Swift	Ditto		96
Samuel Stout	Ditto		3½
Aaron Stiles	Ditto		96
John Scott	Ditto		96
James W. Smith	Corporal		96
Elias Seely	Private		48
Josiah Tuttle	Ditto		51 20
John Toland	Ditto		24
Thomas Van Horne	Ditto		64
Jacob Wrighter	Ditto		360

Making 57 for New Jersey.

A.—Continued.

List of Invalid Pensioners of the United States, belonging to the state of Pennsylvania, and paid at Philadelphia, Pennsylvania, with the annual allowance to each annexed, viz:

		per annum.
Ludiwig Arbigust	Matross	At $96
William Atkinson	Private	72
David Alehouse	Ditto	32
George Attender	Ditto	96
Matthias Anderson	Ditto	96
William Adams	Sergeant	64
David Ackabarger	Private	24
John Alfred	Ditto	96
Isaac Adams	Ditto	48
Jeremiah Archer	Ditto	48
Luke Broadhead	Lieutenant	122 40
Thomas Blair	Ditto	122 40
Jacob Barnitz	Ensign	156
Daniel Baker	Private	96
Jacob Beatun	Ditto	96
James Brannon	Ditto	96
Daniel Buck	Ditto	96
Philip Brenier	Ditto	64

14

A.—Continued.

Name	Rank	At $ 48 per annum.
Jonathan Burwell	Private	At $ 48
George Burton	Ditto	38 40
John Buckell	Ditto	57 60
William Boyd	Ditto	96
Michael Bowman	Ditto	57 60
William Bush	Ditto	96
Jacob Baker	Matross	48
John Brown	Sergeant	64
Walker Baylor	Captain	240
George Benedict	Private	64
Andrew Bartle	Ditto	48
Joseph Bohem	Musician	48
John Burk	Private	32
Jacob Busus	Ditto	72
James Brown	Musician	32
Robert Brown	Sergeant	96
Henry Beach	Private	96
Benjamin Barton	Ditto	72
Frederick Barndollar	Ditto	96
James Barr	Ditto	96
Stephen Barclay	Ditto	96

A.—Continued.

		At $96	per annum.
William Burgess	Private	96	
John Bartholomew	Sergeant	32	
Michael Bird	Musician	96	
Reuben Brinton	Corporal	32	
Samuel Bortfield	Private	32	
John Cambis	Ditto	108 80	
John Clark	Lieutenant	57 60	
Thomas Carney	Private	76 80	
William Campbell	Sergeant	34 12	
Adam Christ	Ditto	44 80	
Robert Chambers	Ditto	64	
William Congleton	Private	57 60	
Alexander Caul	Ditto	57 60	
Alexander Christie	Ditto	48	
Daniel Callahan	Ditto	48	
William Campbell, 2d.	Ditto	57 60	
John Cavenaugh	Ditto	96	
John Cardiffe	Ditto	48	
Josiah Conckling	Ditto	240	
John Crawford	Captain	96	
John Collier	Sergeant		

A.—Continued.

		per annum.
Patrick Collins	Private	At $96
James Cooney	Ditto	96
James Correar	Ditto	48
Stephen Carter	Sergeant	72
Thomas Carty	Private	67 20
James Campbell	Ditto	48
William Cox	Ditto	72
James Curry	Ditto	48
Jeptha Claud	Ditto	48
Jesse Colburn	Sergeant	72
William Carefoot	Private	48
Dennis Coone	Ditto	48
Daniel Coll	Ditto	96
David Cain	Ditto	96
James Conner	Ditto	48
Samuel Carr	Ditto	72
Joseph Chapman	Ditto	32
John Durnall	Ditto	96
Patrick Dempsey	Ditto	96
Michael Duffey	Ditto	64
Henry Doyle	Ditto	57

A.—Continued.

Name	Rank	At $25·60 per annum.
Henry Dougherty	Private	48
William Deevitt	Ditto	57
John Day	Ditto	60
William Deaver	Ditto	64
James Dowling	Ditto	64
James Dysart	Captain	120
Charles Daniels	Private	96
Samuel Deane	Ditto	48
Michael Drury	Ditto	64
David Drum	Ditto	72
George Dugan	Ditto	48
Edward Doyle	Ditto	48
James Dewire	Ditto	96
John Doud	Ditto	96
William Dick	First Lieutenant	204
James Duffield	Private	96
Jonathan De Haven	Ditto	32
James Dyer	Ditto	64
John Downs	Ditto	48
Peter Dempsey	Ditto	48
Henry Duff	Volunteer	72

A.—Continued.

		per annum.
William Devin,	Private	At $48
James Durham	Corporal	96
Samuel Ewing	Ensign	26
James English	Sergeant	96
Joseph Elliott	Private	64
George Earnest	Ditto	67 20
William Edwards	Ditto	96
John Eckhart	Ditto	48
Benjamin Freeman	Sergeant	57 60
John Francis	Private	57 60
John Fogas	Matross	76 80
Jacob Fox	Private	82
Patrick Fowler	Matross	48
Thomas Fream	Sergeant	57 60
John L. Finney	Sergeant major	72
Alexander Foreman	Captain	120
Henry Farbow	Private	48
David Farril	Ditto	96
George Frye	Ditto	72
Benjamin Fennimore	Ditto	96
George W. Ferguson	First lieutenant	204

A.—Continued.

Name	Rank	At $135 per annum
John Fee	Second lieutenant	At $135
Joseph Franklin	Quartermaster sergeant	96
Adam Feathers	Private	48
Thomas Gaskins	Lieutenant	181 33⅓
Philip Gilman	Private	76 80
George Gerlack	Ditto	57 60
John Graaf	Ditto	24
Philip Gibbons	Ditto	72
Alexander Garrett	Ditto	72
Samuel Gilman or Gilmore	Ditto	48
James Glenwoorth	Lieutenant	104
Alexander Gray	Private	76 80
Francis Gallaher	Ditto	96
John Gilbert	Ditto	96
John Gordon	Ditto	96
Daniel Galwick	Sergeant	96
John Gallinger	Private	96
Michael Gallagher	Ditto	96
Thomas Graves	Corporal	32
Robert Guthrie	Private	48
Edward Grant	Ditto	48

A.—Continued.

Name	Rank	At $136 per annum.
Benjamin Hillman	Lieutenant	
William Hebron	Sergeant	96
Valentine Hertzhog	Private	96
Philip Henry	Ditto	96
Patrick Hartney	Ditto	96
Jacob Hartman	Ditto	96
John Haley	Corporal	72
David Hicky	Private	96
Lawrence Hipple	Ditto	48
Peter Hartshill	Ditto	48
William Higginson	Ditto	57 60
David Haney	Ditto	57 60
John Harbeson	Ditto	64
Patrick Hart	Ditto	57 60
Patrick Higgins	Ditto	6½
John Hambell	Ditto	48
Tobias Henery	Ditto	96
Richard Hallowell	Ditto	48
Adam Hartman	Ditto	48
James Huffe	Ditto	96
James Hays	Ditto	6½

A.—Continued.

		At $ 96 per annum.
Cornelius Hendrickson	Private	96
Isaac Hall	Ditto	48
James Irvine	Brigadier general	340
Matthew Jack	Lieutenant	181 33⅓
Thomas Johnson	Ditto	96
David Jackson	Private	76 80
Alexander Irwin	Ditto	48
William Johnson	Ditto	76 80
James Johnson	Ditto	96
Andrew Johnson	Lieutenant	68
Thomas Jenkins	Private	96
Abel Ingram	Sergeant	48
William Jones	Private	96
George W. Jacobs	Third lieutenant	168
Jacob Johnson	Private	48
Gideon Johnson	Ditto	48
James Jones	Musician	96
Thomas Jones	Private	96
John Kesler	Midshipman	32
George Kettle	Private	96
Robert Kearn	Ditto	96

A.—Continued.

		At $57 60 per annum.
Edward Kellen	Private	64
Benjamin Kendrick	Ditto	76 80
John King	Ditto	48
Philip Krugh	Dragoon	48
Anthony Kerns	Private	360
Jonathan Kearsley	Major	48
Allen Kell	Private	72
Joseph Ketler	Ditto	240
Sampson S. King	Captain	48
Nicholas Lott	Sergeant	96
Timothy Lemonton	Ditto	96
John Lalor	Private	96
Henry Love	Ditto	76 80
Isaac Lewis	Ditto	80
David Lyon	Ditto	32
John Leiby	Ditto	24
Miles Lewis	Ditto	48
Samuel Lee	Ditto	64
James Leonard	Ditto	96
Charles Lenox	Ditto	96
Judah Levy	Ditto	96

A.—Continued.

		At $32 per annum.
Joseph Leech	Private	48
William Lake	Ditto	52
Thomas Lyster	Ditto	72
William Latta	Ditto	96
Isaac Leonard	Ditto	72
Jacob Lane	Ditto	48
Daniel Lee	Ditto	74 80
Kenneth M'Koy	Lieutenant	76 80
John Malony	Sergeant	96
John M'Gaughy	Corporal	57 60
Barney M'Guire	Ditto	96
Michael M'Annelly	Gunner	56 20
John M'Pherson	Midshipman	96
James M'Donald	Private	96
Hugh Moore	Ditto	96
Isaiah M'Carty	Ditto	96
Angus M'Ever	Ditto	96
Thomas Moore	Ditto	96
John Manerson	Ditto	96
John Modewell	Ditto	96
Ephraim M'Coy	Ditto	96

A.—Continued.

Name	Rank	At $76 80 per annum.
John Most	Private	76 80
Thomas Mayberry	Ditto	76 80
Samuel M'Clughan	Ditto	76 80
John M'Dermond	Ditto	76 80
Robert Montgomery	Ditto	76 80
James Mathers	Ditto	48
William Murphy	Ditto	48
Thomas M'Fall	Ditto	96
Thomas Monday	Ditto	140 40
Joseph Moorhead	Ensign	96
John Murry	Private	57 60
John M'Conchy	Ditto	240
William M'Kennan	Captain	48
James Moore	Corporal	58 93⅓
Robert M'Clellan	Lieutenant	96
James M'Neal	Private	96
Josiah Magoon	Ditto	176 80
Robert M'Kinney	Lieutenant	6¼
Dennis M'Knight	Private	3¼ 27⅓
Thomas Maze	Ditto	6¼
John Malony	Sergeant	

A.—Continued.

			per annum.
Frederick Matsinger		Private	At $72
John Morrison		Ditto	64
James M'Donald		Ditto	96
James M'Lean		Ditto	48
Hugh Mullen		Ditto	96
Daniel M'Devitt		Ditto	48
Robert Hector M'Pherson		Lieutenant Colonel Brevet	360
Theophilus M'Donald		Private	96
Peter Mavis		Ditto	76 80
John M'Millan		Captain	180
Daniel M'Beth		Private	32
Thomas M'Cloud		Ditto	48
Thomas Morison		Ditto	96
Neal M'Mullen		Ditto	32
George Miller		Ditto	48
William M'Creary		Sergeant	72
Thomas Mellin		Musician	24
John M'Donald		Private	96
Thomas Mullen		Ditto	90
Walter S. Minthorn		Ditto	96
Benjamin Mackey		Ditto	48

A.—Continued.

Name	Rank	At $96 per annum.
James McDade	Private	96
John Neafas	Corporal	38 40
Christian Nagle	Private	96
William Nelson	Ditto	96
Samuel Nesbit	Ditto	72
William Newman	Ditto	48
Andrew Nebinger	Sergeant	48
John Nogle	Private	96
Adam Nethrew	Ditto	96
Joseph Neal	Ditto	38 40
John O'Brian	Ditto	96
Charles O'Brian	Ditto	96
Ichabod O'Brian	Ditto	48
James O'Donnell	Ditto	64
John Purnell	Ditto	96
Joshua Peeling	Sergeant	48
Thomas Park	Corporal	57 60
Frederick Paul	Private	32
Abraham Pyke	Ditto	32
John Pierce	Ditto	64
Peter Partchment	Ditto	

A.—Continued.

		At $48 per annum.
John Peoples	Private	181 33⅓
Thomas Pearson	Lieutenant	57 60
Charles Plemline	Private	6½
Andrew Pinkerton	Ditto	38 40
George Piersoa	Ditto	48
Joshua Patrick	Ditto	96
Alexander Peoples	Ditto	48
William Pringle	Ditto	96
Daniel Prestman	Ditto	48
Amos Pratt	Sergeant	96
William Pritchard	Private	
John Pentland	Captain Brevet Major	300
Lloyd Piott	Private	48
Peter Perry	Ditto	48
Zachariah Reed	Ditto	48
George Richardson	Ditto	76 80
David Richey	Ditto	48
Jacob Rodgers	Ditto	76 80
William Ritchell	Ditto	76 80
Jacob Razor	Ditto	6½
John Rybecker	Ditto	76 80

A.—Continued.

		At $48 per annum.
Griffith Rees	Private	76 80
John Bielly	Ditto	120
Nathan Rawlings	Captain	90 66⅔
William Rice	Lieutenant	48
Hugh Robinson	Private	32
David Roe	Sergeant	72
Samuel Rogers	Private	48
Henry Redlion	Ditto	24
William Rice	Ditto	96
Thomas Rankins	Ditto	48
John Rorhman	Ditto	24
John Russell	Ditto	96
Christian Smith	Ditto	120
Jacob Shartel	Captain	48
Richard Scott	Private	190
Archibald Steel	Lieutenant and adjutant	96
Daniel St. Clair	Drum major	96
Bernard Slaugh	Private	72
John Suring	Ditto	57 60
Samuel Spicer	Ditto	32
John Stiller	Ditto	

A.—Continued.

		At $48 per annum.
Bryant Sloan	Private	At $48
John Shuttz	Ditto	32
Joseph Sapp	Ditto	96
John Stroop	Sergeant	48
Jonas Steel	Private	32
Abraham Storet	Lieutenant	181 33⅓
Francis Smith	Private	48
William Stocker	Ditto	57 60
Peter Swartz	Ditto	48
Alexander Simonton	Sergeant	57 60
John Smith	Private	48
John Robert Shaw	Ditto	96
Christian Stockley	Ditto	64
William Stringfield	Ditto	48
William Scott	Ditto	96
Christopher Scites	Ditto	48
Thomas Scotland	Sergeant	96
John St. Clair	Private	96
John Salter	Ditto	48
John Spencer	Ditto	48
Christian Shoemaker	Ditto	64

A.—Continued.

		per annum.
Martin Shoop alias Shup	Private	At $64
William Stilts	Ditto	64
Thomas B. Stewart	Ditto	96
Seers Shay	Ditto	96
John Smith	Ditto	48
Stephen Singlewood	Sergeant	48
Jeremiah Sullivan	Corporal	48
Conrad Six	Private	32
John Sutton	Ditto	48
William Tomlinson	Ditto	96
John Taylor	Ditto	96
James Tannehill	Ditto	57 60
Thomas Tweedy	Ditto	96
John Thompson	Ditto	96
Richard Taylor	Sergeant	240
Jonathan Tinsley	Private	96
William Thomas	Ditto	96
Obadiah Thomas	Ditto	72
John Tate	Ditto	64
James Thompson	Ditto	19 20
Robert D. Thompson	Ditto	48

A.—Continued.

Name	Rank	per annum.
James Taylor	Private	At $48
John Thimble	Sergeant	48
Elias Ult	Private	32
Enock Varnum	Ditto	96
Thomas Vanderlip	Ditto	72
Lewis Vaughn	Ditto	64
Joseph Vanlaviney	Ditto	76 80
Jonathan Vandergrift	Sergeant	96
Edward Warren	Private	96
Jeremiah Wilson	Ditto	48
Philip Warner	Ditto	38 40
Charles Wallington	Ditto	96
Edward Wade	Ditto	48
John Wight	Sergeant	48
Cal: b Warley	Lieutenant	149 60
George Wolf	Private	72
Robert Wilson	Ensign	39
John Whittington	Private	57 60
Joseph Waters	Ditto	93
Francis White	Lieutenant	90 66⅔
John Wood	Private	48

A.—Continued.

Name	Rank		At $96 per annum.
Andrew Wallace	Sergeant	. . . .	67 20
James Wall	Private	. . . .	72
Samuel Wentz	Ditto	. . . .	95
William Walker	Corporal	. . . .	96
Robert M. Wilson	Private	. . . .	48
Charles Williams	Ditto	. . . .	48
David White	Ditto	. . . .	48
James White	Ditto	. . . .	48
Thomas Young	Ditto	. . . .	96
John Young	Ditto	. . . .	64

Making 406 Invalid Pensioners for Pennsylvania.

A.—Continued.

LIST of Invalid Pensioners of the United States, belonging to the state of Delaware, and paid at New Castle, with the annual allowance to each annexed, viz:

		per annum.
Edward Armstrong	Lieutenant	At $180
Samuel Burchard	Corporal	96
John Clifton	Private	96
Isaac Carrell	Ditto	96
Peter Cunningham	Ditto	64
Patrick Colman	Ditto	96
Isaac Carroll	Ditto	96
William Dolby	Sergeant	96
Stephen Enos	Ditto	48
Joseph Furguson	Private	96
Thomas Holdston	Ditto	96
Nelce Jones	Corporal	48
Thomas D. Lewis	Private	64
Joseph M'Gibbon	Ditto	96

A—Continued.

		At 396 per annum.
John Robinson	Corporal	57 60
John Skilton	Private	360
James Tilton	Physician and surgeon general	48
Thomas Watson	Sergeant	38 40
Hosea Wilson	Private	48
Jesse Watson	Ditto	96
John W. Wilcox	Ditto	

Making 21 Invalid Pensioners for Delaware.

A—Continued.

LIST *of Invalid Pensioners of the United States, belonging to the State of Maryland, and paid at Baltimore, with the annual allowance annexed to each, viz:*

		At $35 20 per annum.
Thomas Green Alvey	Corporal	64
John Anderson	Private	240
Richard Anderson	Captain	48
Robert Alexander	Private	96
John Brown	Sergeant	96
John Byrme	Private	64
James Burk	Ditto	96
James Blever	Ditto	64
Robert Barnet,	Ditto	64
John Bennet	Ditto	67
Thomas Baker	Ditto	64
Charles Buckiup	Ditto	64
Thomas Bishop	Ditto	48
John Boyle	Ditto	240
Perry Benson	Captain	

A—Continued.

Name	Rank	At $240 per annum.
James Bruff	Captain	48
John Brintzal	Private	32
Christian Brown	Ditto	48
James Burk	Ditto	96
William Bannachman	Ditto	48
Martin Bain	Ditto	48
John Bean	Ditto	48
George Beanet	Ditto	48
William Baner	Ditto	48
Daniel Bailey	Ditto	48
Thomas Burns	Ditto	96
Joseph R. Brooks	Second lieutenant	90
Ezekiel Bell	Private	48
James Beatty	Sergeant	52
Malchijah Burk	Pivate	48
Thomas Collember	Ditto	64
Peter Casbury	Private	64
James Current	Ditto	64
Edward Cain	Ditto	48
John Corbett	Ditto	96
John Craig	Ditto	96

A.—Continued.

		At £48 per annum.
Benjamin Coddington	Private	48
George Cozens	Ditto	48
Dominick Cannon	Ditto	72
Henry Cope	Ditto	96
Daniel Callaghan	Ditto	48
Joseph Catherel	Ditto	48
William Collings	Ditto	96
Thomas E. Chesney	Ditto	96
Henry Cable	Ditto	96
James Chalmers	Ditto	96
David Cushwa	Captain	180
John Cator	Private	48
George Cole	Ditto	32
William Clark	Ditto	48
George Collins	Corporal	32
John Chalk	Private	32
Charles Dowd	Corporal	96
Barnabas Doughty	Private	64
John Davis	Ditto	64
James Davidson	Ditto	96
William Dalrymple	Ditto	48

A.—Continued.

Name	Rank	At $ per annum.
John Duncan	Private	96
Richard Diffendaffer	Sergeant	48
Henry Duffy	Private	48
Robert Davis	Ditto	48
Nelson Davidson	First sergeant	48
Elijah Dailey	Private	64
William Down	Ditto	96
James Danford	Ditto	96
Lawrence Everhart	Sergeant	96
William Evans	Private	64
John L. Elbert	Lieutenant	1:2
John Essender	Private	48
Thomas Edmondson	Ditto	48
Conrad Euler	Ditto	48
George Finleyson	Ditto	64
Dennis Flannaghan	Ditto	64
Philip Fisher	Ditto	64
Simon Fogler	Ditto	32
John Ferguson	Ditto	96
John French	Matross	96
Samuel Foy	Private	96

A—Continued.

Name	Rank	At $48 per annum.
Benjamin Flowers	Private	At $48
James Fagan	Ditto	48
William Fannon	Ditto	48
Benjamin Fleetwood	Ditto	48
James Fulton	Ditto	48
James Garth	Ditto	64
John Gambare	Ditto	64
William Green	Ditto	64
Abraham Gamble	Ditto	96
Walter Golden	Ditto	48
William Gray	Ditto	96
Jarred Gossage	Ditto	96
John Gidleman	Ditto	48
James Gibson	Ditto	72
Thomas Gaddl	Ditto	48
Charles Goddard	Ditto	72
William Guthrie	Ditto	24
Richard Harden	Sergeant	96
John Howard	Private	64
Samuel Huggins	Ditto	64
William Hurly	Ditto.	64

A.—Continued.

Name	Rank	At $64 per annum.
Edward Hood	Private	32
Samuel Hinnis	Ditto	64
Samuel Harris	Ditto	48
Jose Hvatt	Ditto	96
William Happy	Ditto	96
Thomas Hill	Ditto	64
Barney Havs	Ditto	96
Francis Hutchinson	Ditto	96
George W. Howard	Sergeant	96
James Herron	Private	40
Patrick Handlin	Gunner	64
Alexander Jones	Private	96
John Jonas	Ditto	64
James Isaacs	Ditto	64
Benedict Johnson	Ditto	67 20
John Johnson	Ditto	96
Robert Jenkins	Matross	96
Peter W. Johnson	Private	32
Joshua Jones	Ditto	96
Samuel Jordan	Ditto	96
Edward Joy	Ditto	96

A.—Continued.

		per annum.
Richard Kisby	Private	At $76 80
Robert Kearns	Sergeant	96
John Kirkpatrick	Private	76 80
Thomas King	Ditto	57 60
Edward Kean	Ditto	96
William Keough	Ditto	96
John Kearnes	Ditto	96
William Kelly	Sergeant	96
Emanuel Kent	Private	96
John Klee	Sergeant	32
Conrad Keller	Ditto	48
William Keen, jun.	Private	96
John Kirby	Ensign	117
Christopher Lambert	Private	64
John Lowry	Ditto	64
Edward Leary	Ditto	96
Patrick Logan	Ditto	48
Jesse Lazarino	Ditto	48
Philip Lawless	Ditto	64
Joseph Lutz	Ditto	48
Thomas Le Mark	Ditto.	72

A.—Continued.

		At $ 96 per annum.
Emery Lowman	Private	96
John Levering	Ditto	32
William Lynch	Ditto	48
John Lamb	Ditto	96
John Lawless	Ditto	32
John Lamb	Ditto	96
Mathias Loughgushi	Ditto	24
Abraham Larew	Ditto	48
Jeremiah Mudd	Sergeant	96
John Mathews	Corporal	70 40
John M'Coy	Private	96
Michael M'Guire	Ditto	64
Hugh M'Leod	Ditto	64
John Meek	Ditto	64
William Mooney	Ditto	96
Daniel M'Carty	Matross	96
Jonathan Morris	Captain	120
James M'Gahee	Private	48
James M'Laughlin	Ditto	72
William M'Elvins	Ditto	72
Jeremiah Malony	Corporal	48

A.—Continued.

		per annum.
James M'Neal	Private	At $96
James W. M'Cullock	Corporal	96
William H. Murray	Sergeant	96
John D. Mosyer	Private	48
Isaac Morrow	Ditto	64
Henry Magauren	Ditto	48
Henry Marsh	Ditto	32
Lewis Mason	Ditto	64
William A. Needham	Sergeant	96
John Nye	Private	96
Theophilus I Norton	Sergeant	96
Stokely Newman	Private	48
James Nowell	Ditto	96
Luther A. Norris	Ditto	96
Jacob Nell	Ditto	76 80
Daniel W. Norris	Sergeant	60
John Neal	Private	48
James O'Hara	Ditto	64
Joseph O'Guire	Ditto	64
John O'Hard	Ditto	96
Joseph Owens	Sergeant	24

A.—Continued.

		per annum.
William O'Neal	Private	At $48
Elisha Oldham	Ditto	48
Barney O'Donnell	Ditto	96
James Pope	Ditto	6¼
Joseph Polhemus	Ditto	6¼
Antone Pilsch	Ditto	96
Charles Parker	Ditto	48
John Pigeon	Ditto	48
Samuel L. Payne	Ditto	96
William Perry	Ditto	48
Thomas Parsons	Ditto	32
Christopher Riend	Ditto	64
William Rogers	Ditto	6¼
Charles Robinson	Ditto	64
Michael Roe	Ditto	64
Joseph Richardson	Ditto	48
Joseph Russel	Ditto	38 40
Christopher Reed	Ditto	6¼
Jacob Redenour	Ditto	96
John Repp	Rifle Corps	48
Ichariah Roberts	Private	24

A.—Continued.

Name	Rank	per annum.
John Reese	Lieutenant	
George Reintzel	Private	At $68 72
Thomas Robinson	Ditto	96
John Reed	Ditto	48
David Richards	Ditto	48
John Robinson	Ditto	32
Frederick Reinecke	Ditto	48
George Reppart	Ditto	48
Thomas Sherwood	Ditto	57 60
James Scott	Sergeant	39 16¾
John Snider	Corporal	70 40
Thomas Saunders	Private	64 83¼
William Slye	Ditto	64
Jacob Shandy	Ditto	64
Philip Sullivan	Ditto	64
John Shovell	Ditto	64
Philip Shoebrook	Ditto	64
James Smith	Ditto	64
Daniel Smith	Ditto	64
James Smith	Ditto	64
David Smith	Ditto	64

A.—Continued

		per annum.
Joseph Smith	Private	At $64
Valentine Smith	Ditto	64
Valentine Smith	Ditto	32
James Smith	Ditto	76 80
James Sewall	Ditto	96
George Scoone	Corporal	48
John Simpson	Private	48
Daniel Shane	Ditto	96
Thomas Skivington	Ditto	96
John Stockton	Ditto	64
John Stewart	Driver	32
David Stottlemyer of David	Corporal	48
Joseph Stansbury	Private	48
John N. Stewart	Ditto	32
James Tillard	Ditto	64 83½
John Trisner	Ditto	64
Henry Tomm	Ditto	48
John Cocke Tyler	Ditto	48
Samuel Tanner	Ditto	48
Levi Tarr	Ditto	48
William Thomson	Ditto	48

A.—Continued.

Name	Rank	At $48 per annum.
Aquila Tulley	Private	48
Zachariah Urie	Ditto	96
George Vaughn	Lieutenant	181 33⅓
Nathaniel Whaler	Private	96
John Wills	Ditto	64
Richard Wilkerson	Ditto	64
Mark Walsh	Ditto	64
James White	Ditto	96
Samuel B. White	Ditto	96
Michael Waltman	Ditto	64
James Watts	Corporal	96
William J. Williams	Sergeant	96
John Willis	Ditto	48
John Weaver	Ensign	52
Horatio Weedon	Private	32
Martin Wisbaugh	Ditto	48
James Wells	Sergeant	96
Amos A. Williams	Private	32
Nathaniel Williams	Ditto	64
Benjamin Walker	Ditto	32

A.—Continued.

		At $96 per annum.
Josiah Westlake	Private -	At $96
Stephen Yoe	Sergeant -	96
Thomas Yates	Private -	64

Making 269 Invalid Pensioners for Maryland.

A,—Continued.

List of Invalid Pensioners of the United States, belonging to the state of Virginia, and paid at Richmond, with the annual allowance to each annexed, viz:

		per annum.
James Askew	Private	At $64
John Angill	Ditto	64
John Aiken	Ditto	64
Matthew Amicks	Ditto	48
Edward Absolom	Ditto	96
Charles Atwell	Ditto	48
William Bradly	Sergeant	96
Robert Burchett	Ditto	96
Robert Beckham	Ditto	80
Alexander Bunton	Ditto	64
Bazel Brown	Ditto	64
Thomas Brown	Ditto	64
Alexander Bonny, or Bonnal	Ditto	53 33⅓
Francis Boyd	Ditto	53 33⅓
George Black	Ditto	53 33⅓
Thomas Booth	Ditto	32
William Butler	Ditto	76 80
Joseph Biggs	Ensign	120 40

A,—Continued.

Name	Rank	At $76 80 per annum.
James Braxton	Private	64½
David Blew	Ditto	64
William Barber	Ditto	96
John Berry	Ditto	96
John Burton	Sergeant	156
Daniel Ball	Ensign	
William Burke	Private	6½
Samuel Burton	Ditto	48
James Buxton	Lieutenant	76 80
William Burke	Private	48
James Batson	Ditto	57 60
James Bridget	Ditto	48
Timothy Bray	Ditto	32
Thomas Behaw	Ditto	32
Richard Buchanan	Ditto	96
David Buchan	Ditto	96
John Brown	Ditto	32
Gray Barber	Ditto	48
William Bishop	Ditto	64
Glover Baker	Ditto	24
Simon Bright	Ditto	96

A.—Continued.

		per annum.
		At $120
Richard H. Bell	Captain	
John Crookshanky	Private	48
George Cress	Ditto	48
James Campbell	Lieutenant	120
Thomas Clark	Sergeant	96
Bartlett Coxe	Private	96
Miles Cardiff	Ditto	96
Leonard Cooper	Captain	166 66
James Chambers	Private	96
Francis Combs	Ditto	80
Archibald Compton	Ditto	64
Laurence Corner	Ditto	64
James Cottman	Ditto	53 82
John Corbett	Ditto	32
John Collings	Ditto	24
Henry Crook	Ditto	64
Thomas Coverly	Ensign	156
Isaiah Corbin	Private	48
John Crute	Lieutenant	176 80
John Carmichael	Private	96
Leonard Clark	Ditto	96

A.—Continued.

Name	Rank	At $48 per annum.
David Craig	Private	57 60
David Callis	Ditto	96
Ischamer De Graffenriedt	Ditto	64
James Davenport	Ditto	64
Abraham Davis	Ditto	64
Patrick Daugherty	Ditto	42 64
James Durham	Ditto	72
Joshua Davidson	Dragoon	96
Jonathan Byer	Private	60
John Davis	Sergeant	96
Grieve Drummond	Private	96
Robert Darrah	Sergean	48
James Daugherty	Private	72
Thomas Donnelly	Ditto	168
James J Denoon	Third lieutenant	64
Elijah Estis	Private	42 64
Reuben Earthen	Ditto	108 80
William Evans	Lieutenant	38 40
Thomas Eastman	Private	24
William Eaty	Ditto	42 64
William Francis	Ditto	

A.—Continued.

	Rank	At £42 64 per annum.
Frederick Finder	Private	204
Thomas Fenn	Captain M.	96
Thomas Flint	Private	64
Richard Fling	Ditto	96
Albion Gordon	Quartermaster sergeant	80
Martin Griffin	Private	64
Patrick Glasson	Ditto	53 32
Joseph Gardner	Ditto	64
Griffin Griffith	Ditto	64
James Gleason	Ditto	38 40
Patrick Gass	Ditto	96
Paul Hagarty	Ditto	64
John Hughes	Sergeant	96
William Hubbard	Ditto	96
Samuel Hunt	Private	96
Peter Howard	Ditto	64
John Halfperny	Ditto	64
James Hamilton	Ditto	53 32
Bartlett Hawkins	Ditto	96
Henry Hurst	Ditto	48
Elijah Hedges	Ditto	96

19

A.—Continued.

		At $48 per annum.
Fielding Harding	Sergeant	At $48
Henry Hall	Private	96
John Holdcombe	Captain	180
James Howard	Private	48
Nathaniel Henry	Lieutenant	204
George Hill	Private	62 40
Edward Heartwell	Ditto	48
Robert Holbert	Ditto	96
William Harrison	Ditto	48
James Hamilton	Ditto	96
John Herrington	Sergeant	96
John Haney	Private	48
Calvin Hurd	Corporal	48
Thomas S. Hutchins	Sergeant	72
Richard Joy	Private	80
William Jones	Ditto	64
Thomas Jorden	Ditto	64
John Jeffries	Ditto	57 60
William Jones, 2d.	Ditto	96
John Jordan	Lieutenant	102
Samuel Kirkpatrick	Private	64

A.—Continued.

Name	Rank	At $ 64 per annum.
Michael Kinson	Private	At $ 64
Charles Kirk	Ditto	48
Robert Leonard	Ditto	72
Andrew Lewis	Ditto	96
Joseph Lijon	Ditto	57 60
Newman Landman	Dragoon	64
John Long	Private	48
Henry Long	Ditto	32
Wyatt Lathrop	Ditto	48
Charles Love	Ditto	96
Martin Murphy	Sergeant	96
James Murphey	Private	96
William Moore	Ditto	96
John Morris	Ditto	96
John M'Clennen	Ditto	96
Richard Murray	Ditto	64
Joseph Miles	Ditto	64
Banks Moody	Ditto	42 66
Andrew M'Guire	Ditto	96
Peter Mason	Ditto	32
William Morgan	Seaman	76 80

A.—Continued.

Name	Rank			At $240 per annum.
Simon Morgan	Captain	•	•	
William M‘Clennahan	Private	•	•	48
John Martin	Sergeant	•	•	48
John M‘Chesney	Private	•	•	64
Daniel M‘Carty	Ditto	•	•	76 80
James M‘Cray	Ditto	•	•	32
James M‘Laughlin	Ditto	•	•	96
John M‘Donald	Ditto	•	•	96
William Morgan, 2d.	Ditto	•	•	96
Robert Marchbank	Ditto	•	•	96
John Newman	Ditto	•	•	96
Abraham Nettles	Ditto	•	•	64
John Newman	Sergeant	•	•	57 60
Timothy O‘Connor	Private	•	•	64
Dennis O‘Farrall	Ditto	•	•	42 66
William Oversticel	Ditto	•	•	57 60
Henry Overly	Ditto	•	•	96
William Peak	Sergeant	•	•	96
George Pittman	Ditto	•	•	96
William Parmer	Corporal	•	•	80
Thomas Philips	Private	•	•	96

A.—Continued.

Name	Rank				per annum.
John Proctor	Private	. .	. .	. .	At $64
Jacob Price	Ditto				64
John Powell	Sergeant				64
Reuben Plunkitt	Private				48
John Peters	Ditto				48
Thomas Parkinson	Ditto				48
Thomas Pettus	Ditto				48
William D. Phielding	Ditto				48
Robert Reading	Ditto				96
John Ryan	Ditto				64
James Rogers	Ditto				64
Charles Robertson	Ditto				53 32
James Robertson	Ditto				42 66
Nathan Rowland	Ditto				32
William Reading	Ditto				64
Peter Rust	Ditto				53 32
John Rearden	Ditto				64
Daniel Rady	Ditto				48
Evan Rayland	Ditto				57 60
Thomas Rogers	Ditto				48
Willis Rumsey	Ditto				48

A.—Continued.

Name	Rank				At $48 per annum.
William Richards	Private	.	.	.	240
David Scott	Captain	.	.	.	96
John Seamster	Private	.	.	.	96
David Steele	Ditto	.	.	.	80
William Simmonds	Ditto	.	.	.	80
Joseph Sandridge	Ditto	.	.	.	64
William Stricker	Ditto	.	.	.	64
John Smith, 7th. regiment	Ditto	.	.	.	64
John Smith, 8th. ditto	Ditto	.	.	.	64
John Stadner	Ditto	.	.	.	64
Smith Stephens	Ditto	.	.	.	64
Joseph Scars	Ditto	.	.	.	53 32
Daniel Smith	Ditto	.	.	.	76 80
Samuel Swearingen	Ditto	.	.	.	48
Benjamin Sadler	Ditto	.	.	.	57 60
Benjamin Strother	Dragoon	.	.	.	64
Jacob Seay	Private	.	.	.	96
Charles Swead	Ditto	.	.	.	67 20
William Stanley	Ditto	.	.	.	32
George Sparling	Ditto	.	.	.	96
Thomas Thweat	Captain	.	.	.	240

A.—Continued.

		At $96 per annum
Thomas Trent	Sergeant	96
Thomas Toms	Private	64
James Taylor	Ditto	64
Stephen Terry	Ditto	64
John Thorp	Ditto	57 60
Edward Tuck	Ditto	48
Vincent Tapp	Sergeant	48
Benjamin Tyler	Private	64
Alexander Turner	Ditto	48
Thomas Tinsbloom	Ditto	48
Reuben Thacker	Ditto	96
Peter Vaughn	Ditto	181 33
Robert White	Lieutenant	160
Willis Wilson	Ditto	80
Enoch Wallace	Sergeant	96
Jacob Wine	Private	80
Robert Williams	Ditto	64
Joseph Watkins	Ditto	64
William Willeburne	Ditto	64
Jesse Witt	Ditto	64
John Whitlock	Ditto	64

A—Continued.

		At $72 per annum.
Joseph White	Private	96
Henry Williams	Ditto	96
George Walton	Ditto	72
Samuel Walker	Ditto	96
Thomas Wheeler	Ditto	96
James Wright	Ditto	48
Fielding Williams	Ditto	96
Henry J Williams	Ditto	72
Lewis Woolbanks	Ditto	80
John Yeager	Ditto	32
Joshua Younger	Ditto	64
John Yardley	Ditto	

Making 240 Invalid Pensioners for Virginia.

A—Continued.

LIST of Invalid Pensioners of the United States, belonging to the State of North Carolina, and paid at Fayetteville, N. C. with the annual allowance to each annexed, viz:

		per annum.
James Ames	Private	At $96
William Avis	Ditto	48
George Bledsoe	Ditto	96
Isaac Bates	Ditto	67 20
John Baxter	Ditto	57 60
Charles Butler	Ditto	57 60
Thomas Belsiah	Ditto	96
Warren Benton	Ditto	48
Benjamin Boulton	Ditto	72
Thomas Chiles	Captain	160
James Carrigan	Private	57 60
Samuel Carter	Ditto	19 20
Braxton Carter	Ditto	57 60
Alston Cook	Ditto	96
John Chittim	Ditto	72

A.—Continued.

Name	Rank	At $96 per annum.
James Christian	Private	48
Samuel Espy	Ditto	67 20
Charles Ellam	Ditto	67 20
William Eaton	Sergeant	48
David Flanagan	Private	38 40
Samuel Freeman	Ditto	48
William Fields	Ditto	72
John Frazier	Ditto	96
Alston Fort	Ditto	64
Herman Garkins	Ditto	57 60
John Gillon	Ditto	96
Richard Gressum	Ditto	48
Thomas Goodrum	Ditto	96
Miles Goforth	Ditto	180
Thomas Harris	Major	96
Elisha Hunt	Private	96
Wyat Hinckley	Ditto	180
James Houston	Captain	57 60
Daniel Houston	Private	57 60
Howell Harton	Ditto	86 40
Elias House	Ditto	

A.—Continued.

				At $67 20 per annum.
Alexander Haynes			Private	96
William Hall			Ditto	32
Uriah Hudson			Ditto	96
David Johnson			Ditto	57 60
Francis Johnson			Ditto	96
Samuel Johnson			Ditto	48
William Jones			Ditto	32
Thomas Jacobs			Ditto	57 60
Isaac Kennedy			Ditto	48
Elijah Kidwell			Ditto	48
James Larremore			Ditto	48
Amos Lewis			Ditto	64
William Lefever			Ditto	76 80
William Liles			Ditto	96
Alexander Morrison			Sergeant	120
Daniel M‘Kissick			Captain	57 60
Thomas M Kissick			Private	64
David Miller			Ditto	67 20
Edmund M‘Kinney			Ditto	48
William Martin			Ditto	32
Charles M‘Lain			Ditto	

A.—Continued.

		per annum.
Sullivan Newell	Private	At $72
James Porter	Ditto	28 40
James Potts	Ditto	28 40
James Parks	Ditto	64
John Pierce	Ditto	96
Daniel Perry	Ditto	32
John Pattason	Ditto	48
Stephen Pitts	Ditto	48
Jesse Rigsby	Ditto	64
Humphry Rogers	Ditto	96
James Redfern	Ditto	57 16
Michael Reep	Ditto	48
John Sweeney	Ditto	96
Thomas Smith	Ditto	96
James Smith	Ditto	96
Ithamar Singletary	Sergeant	24
William Smith	Private	96
Hugh Stanly	Ditto	64
John Spears	Ditto	57 16
Thomas Smith	Ditto	48
George Smitteel	Ditto	32

A—Continued.

		At $96 per annum.
Philip Thomas	Sergeant	96
Maltiah Turner	Pivate	64
Joel Terrell	Ditto	57 16
Benjamin Vickery	Private	32
John Wilfong	Ditto	57 16
John Wentz	Ditto	48
Henry Williams	Ditto	72
Benjamin Ward	Ditto	48
Thomas Washburn	Ditto	

87 Invalid Pensioners for North Carolina.

A.—Continued.

LIST of *Invalid Pensioners of the United States, belonging to the state of South Carolina, and paid at the Branch Bank U. States, Charleston, South Carolina, viz:*

			per annum.
			At $96
James Armstrong	. . . .	. . . .	6¼
John Alverson	. . . .	Private .	24 12
John Calhoun	. . . .	Ditto .	48
Joseph Clark	. . . .	Ditto .	24 12
William Dunlap	. . . .	Ditto .	48
Joseph Davidson	. . . .	Ditto .	96
Robert Darrah	. . . .	Sergeant	57 16
Joshua Hawkins	. . . .	Private .	96
Lewis Howland	. . . .	Ditto .	63 96
Sion Holly	. . . .	Ditto .	76 80
Malcolm Keys	. . . .	Ditto .	96
Joseph Kerr	. . . .	Ditto .	48
Joseph King	. . . .	Ditto .	24 12
John Loony	. . . .	Ditto .	144
Joseph M'Junkin	. . . .	Major .	

A—Continued.

		At $24 12 per annum.
Andrew M'Allister	Private	
John Martin	Ditto	48
William Moore	Ditto	48
Samuel Otterson	Captain	95
Daniel Odom	Private	89 8
Samuel Rose	Ditto	32
Jasper Tomiton	Ditto	48

22 Invalid Pensioners for South Carolina.

A.—Continued.

LIST of Invalid Pensioners of the U. States, belonging to the state of Georgia, and paid at the Branch Bank U. States, at Savannah, Georgia, viz:

		per annum.
William Andreson	Sergeant -	At $96
Herman Bird	Private -	48
Daniel Conner	Lieutenant	181 32
Alexander Cameron	Private	48
Austin Daboev	Ditto	96
Charles Damson	Ditto	96
James P. Edmonston	Ditto	80
Benjamin Fry	Ditto	96
Thomas Green	Ditto	48
John Guthrie	Ditto	48
John Garner	Ditto	48
Edward Griffin	Ditto	24 12
Reuben Goolsby	Ditto	48
John Hunt	Ditto	72
Richard Henderson	Ditto	96

A—Continued.

			per annum.
Harrison Jones	Private	- -	At $80
Henry Kerr	Captain	- -	120
Daniel M'Elduff	Lieutenant	- -	181 52
Joshua Mercer	Private	- -	48
Robert Niel	Captain -	, ,	96
Seybert Odum	Private -	, ,	96
William Penticost	Lieutenant	- -	60
John Shackleford	Private -	- -	64
James Shirley	Ditto -	- -	96
Presley Thornton	Corporal	- -	48
Samuel Whately	Private -	- -	96

25 Invalid Pensioners for Georgia.

21

A.—Continued.

LIST of Invalid Pensioners of the United States, belonging to the state of Kentucky, and paid at Lexington, with the annual allowance to each annexed, viz:

Andrew Allison	Private	At $57 60 per annum.
William Arnold	Lieutenant	48
Squire Boone	Private	57 60
James Berry	Ditto	32
John Brown	Sergeant	48
William Berry	Private	96
John Brown	Ditto	64
Dennis Belt	Ditto	72
Daniel V. Bealmear	Corporal	48
Richard Bawlin	Artificer	72
William Cook	Private	48
James Curtis	Ditto	48
Roger Cooper	Ditto	48
Zacheus Cord	First Lieutenant	204
William Carter	Private	63 96

A.—Continued.

Name	Rank			At $48 per annum.
John Campbell	Sergeant	. .	. .	96
Enock Ducher	Private	. .	. .	96
Spencer Darbell	Ditto	. .	. .	96
James S. Davis	Ditto	. .	. .	96
James Devourix	Ditto	. .	. .	48
Henry Doherty, or Daugherty	Corporal	. .	. .	48
James Dougherty	Private	. .	. .	72
Abraham Estes	Ditto	. .	. .	64
Robert Elder	Ditto	. .	. .	96
Wilham English	Ditto	. .	. .	72
Clement Estes	Corporal	. .	. .	96
John Fury	Private	. .	. .	64
Joseph Frost	Ditto	. .	. .	32
Andrew Green	Ditto	. .	. .	240
Isaac Gray	Captain	. .	. .	96
Jesse P. Green	Private	. .	. .	38 40
Thomas Hickman	Ditto	. .	. .	48
Henry Hawkins	Ditto	. .	. .	48
Lemuel Hewlit	Ditto	. .	. .	48
Daniel Hailey	Ditto	. .	. .	48
John Hinkson	Ditto	. .	. .	48

A—Continued.

		per annum.
George Hendrick	Private	At $48
Elkana Hendley	Ditto	32
John Jacobs	Ditto	96
John Jourdan	Ditto	96
Leroy Jones	Ditto	63 84
John Kersner	Ditto	64
John King	Ditto	96
Thomas Knowles	Ditto	96
William Little	Ditto	48
Francis Lee	Corporal	96
Thompson C. Lloyd	Sergeant	32
Quintin Moore	Private	32
Samuel Marchead	Ditto	48
John M'Kinney	Virginia state pensioner	96
John M'Clure	Private	48
George Manwaring	Ditto	96
Thomas M Barney	Ditto	57 60
Peter Murphy	Ditto	72
William Nieves	Ditto	48
Alexander Naismith	Ditto	48
Samuel Newell	Lieutenant	108 80

A.—Continued.

Name			Rank	At $ 48 per annum
Virgil Poe	.	.	Private	48
William Pennington	.	.	Ditto	96
Joseph Paxton	.	.	Ditto	48
Thomas Robertson	.	.	Ditto	96
Charles Rumsey	.	.	Ditto	96
Benjamin Raynes	.	.	Ditto	96
Henry Shaw	.	.	Ditto	48
John Shanks	.	.	Ditto	64
Joseph Shaw	.	.	Ditto	38 40
George Shannon	.	.	Indian conductor	144
Andrew Salisbury	.	.	Private	72
Jeremiah Searcy	.	.	Ditto	96
Eli Short	.	.	Assistant forage master	117
Samuel Sharron	.	.	Private	48
Page Shields	.	.	Ditto	64
John Shuffield	.	.	Ditto	48
William Sutherland	.	.	Ditto	32
John Shaw	.	.	Ditto	96
Francis L. Slaughter	.	.	Ditto	57 60
Edward Stivers	.	.	Musician	96
William Simson	.	.	Private	48

A.—Continued.

		At $72	per annum.
Spencer Shoemate	Private	48	
James Stewart	Ditto	48	
George Tennell	Ditto	38 40	
Joseph Todd	Ditto	24	
Willis Tandy	Ditto	72	
Julius Tuner	Ditto	96	
William Turner	Corporal	300	
Richard Taylor	Captain	64	
James Warson	Private	48	
Samuel W. White	Ditto	48	
Thomas Williams	Ditto	48	
John Ward	Ditto	84	
Armistead Whitehead	Third Lieutenant	96	
Joseph Wilkinson	Ships' corporal	96	
Robert Worrel	Private	48	
William Wilson	Ditto		

Making 94 for Kentucky.

A.—Continued.

List of Invalid Pensioners of the United States, belonging to the state of Tennessee, and paid at Nashville, with the annual allowance to each annexed, viz:

		per annum.
		At $48
William Abney	Private	
Benjamin Blackburn	Ditto	96
John Blair	Lieutenant	108 80
John Bell	Ditto	136
Joseph Brooks	Corporal	96
Edmund Borum	Private	96
John Bruce	Ditto	72
John Berry	Ditto	48
James Basford	Ditto	96
James Barr	Ditto	48
William Carr	Ditto	48
James Crawford	Ensign	93 60
Ethelred Cobb	Private	48
John Caldwell	Ditto	64
William Dennie	Ditto	72
Robert C. Davis	Ditto	72

A.—Continued.

			per annum.
Bracket Davison	Private	. . . . .	At $72
James Dunlap	Ditto	. . . . .	96
Drury Easely	Ditto	. . . . .	72
Robert Elliott	Ditto	. . . . .	96
Perry Floyd	Ditto	. . . . .	48
John Fain	Ditto	. . . .	76 80
Alfred Flournoy	Third Lieutenant		168
Isaac Fancher	Private		48
Joseph Gilmore	Ditto	.	33 60
William Gann	Ditto		96
Alexander M. Gray	Ditto		96
Bailey Goodsey	Sergeant		48
Rinley Hazelet	Private		96
William Haile	Ditto		32
John Huddleston	Ditto		56
Jacob House	Ditto		96
David Hubbard	Ditto		48
Hugh Hays	Ditto		48
Wiley V. Harper	Corporal		72
Gideon Harmon	Private		48
Abner Johnson	Ditto		96

A.—Continued.

		At $48 per annum.
Charles Kilgore	Private	48
John Kirk	Ditto	48
Darby Mars	Ditto	96
Joseph Morrissit	Ditto	48
Gideon Mills	Ditto	96
Payton Madison	Ditto	96
John Madison	Corporal	96
James Montgomery	Private	48
Jesse M'Annally	Sergeant	96
Mark Miller	Private	48
Richard Martin	Ditto	48
Archibald M'Donald	Ditto	96
John Newman	Captain	120
George Nelson	Corporal	96
James Newbury	Private	48
Harrison Posey	Fifer	64
John Pritchett	Private	72
Joseph Reed	Ditto	64
James Russell	Ditto	64
Daniel Ruminer	Ditto	72
Luna Rhea	Ditto	96

A.—Continued.

		per annum.
John Russell	Private	At $48
Thomas Reynold	Sergeant	96
Benjamin Reynolds	Captain	240
James Shaw	Private	96
William L. Sypert	Ditto	48
Samuel Scott	Ditto	90
George Sieeker	Ditto	72
W. I Shumate	Lieutenant	168
Eli Sawyer	Private	32
Prestley Shepherd	Ditto	32
Nathaniel Smith	First lieutenant	153
Lockey Simpson	Private	24
John Taylor	Ditto	72
Grant Taylor	Ditto	96
John V. Thorp	Corporal	32
John Thornburgh	Sergeant	48
William Tipton	Private	96
Reuben Thomas	Ditto	48
Stephen Thomas	Ditto	72
Thomas Wyatt	Ditto	48
William Wright	Ditto	

A.—Continued.

		At $240 per annum.
Beverly Williams	Captain	240
Mathew Williams	Private	72
Samuel Wheeler	Ditto	48
David Waddle	Corporal	96
David Wills	Sergeant	72

Making 84 for Tennessee.

A.—Continued.

LIST of Invalid Pensioners of the United States, belonging to the state of Ohio, and paid at Chilicothe, with the annual allowance to each annexed, viz:

Name	Rank	per annum.
George Adams	Private	At $96
Benjamin Armstrong	Ditto	96
Bartholemew Berry	Ditto	96
Humphrey Beckett	Ditto	48
Joshua Bennet	Ditto	96
William Bowyer	Ditto	96
Thomas Baldwin	Ditto	96
Paul Bonnel	Ditto	48
William Brinton	Ditto	72
Andrew Bushnell	Second lieutenant	45
Enock Barnum	Private	96
Malyne Baker	Ditto	48
Robert Barron	Ditto	96
Oliver Bennett	Ditto	96
George Barngrover	Ditto	96
Charles Blach	Ditto	48
John Calhoun	Captain	180
James Critchton	Private	96

A.—Continued.

			At $48 per annum.
Elijah Chinraworth	Private	.	At $48
Daniel C. Carter	Ditto	.	48
George Cassidy	Ditto	.	96
Charles Cissna	Second lieutenant		180
George Culins	Private	.	48
Robert Cue	Ditto	.	48
Stephen Cissney	Ditto	.	48
Johnson Cook	Sergeant		48
Willis Copelan	Private	.	48
Benjamin Daniels	Major	.	300
Jeremiah Douglass	Private	.	96
Jesse Downs	Ditto	.	48
Thomas Dowler	Ditto	.	32
Daniel Davis	Sergeant		64
Robert Doing	Corporal	.	96
Walter Dixon	Private	.	32
James Elwell	Corporal		48
Joseph England	Private	.	96
Moses Eldred	Ditto	.	64
Daniel Fielding	Sergeant militia	.	64
Ira L. Foster	Private	.	48

A.—Continued.

Name	Rank	per annum.
John Fay	Private	At $96
Thomas Fugate	Ditto	96
Jacob Frank	Ditto	32
James Foster	Sergeant	48
Benjamin Fickle	Lieutenant	204
James Gallespie	Private	76 80
Younger Grady	Ditto	57 60
Abner Gage	Ditto	96
Elisha B. Green	Sergeant	96
Isaac Green	Private	48
Samuel Hawkins	Mounted volunteer	64
George Hartsell	Private	32
Samuel Hall	Ditto	96
David Harr	Ditto	96
John Hamilton	Captain	120
Clayton Harper	Private	6¼
James Jarvis	Ditto	72
Jacob Kendelsperyer	Ditto	48
David Kirkland	Sergeant	48
Dennis Laughlan	Private	48
James Munn	Captain	120

A.—Continued.

		At £96 per annum.
Edward Miller	Sergeant Major -	48
Robert M'Cullock	Sergeant -	64
Cornelius M'Mahon	Private -	270
John R. Martin	Hospital surgeon's mate	64
Samuel M'Kenny	Private	96
John J. Mahanna	Ditto	96
Michael M'Dermot	Ditto	32
William M'Intosh	Ditto	48
William Maxwell	Ditto	48
Charles Mullin	Ditto	48
Samuel Miller	Ditto	96
William Morrow	Ditto	48
John Norton	Ditto	135
Alexander Patterson	Second Lieutenant	48
Matthew Patterson	Private	300
Robert Patterson	Colonel -	360
William Piatt	Ditto	72
Martin Rohrer	Sergeant	48
Minny Ryneason	Private	48
James Rankin	Ditto	48
William Rhodes	Ditto	

A.—Continued.

Name	Rank			At $96 per annum.
Joseph N. Ross	Sergeant			At $96
Michael Stephens	Private			48
William Sibberal	Ditto			96
Samuel Still	Sergeant			6¼
Zebedee Smith	Private			96
John Symmonds	Corporal			48
Peter Shipled	Private			72
John Sprague	Ditto			72
William Snyder	Ditto			72
Robert Smith	Ditto			96
Andrew Stewart	Ditto			96
Daniel Swyers	Ditto			96
Aaron Stewart	Ditto			48
Daniel Stagg	Ditto			96
William Vineyard	Ditto			48
Robert Williams	Ditto			96
William Wells	Captain			240
James C. Wingard	Sergeant			2⅜

Making 99 for Ohio.

A.—Continued.

LIST of Invalid Pensioners of the U. States, belonging to the state of Louisiana, and paid at New Orleans, with the annual allowance to each annexed, viz:

		per annum.
Amos Avery	Private	At $ 48
James Allen	Ditto	48
Alexis Andry	Ditto	96
Jean Du Peron	Ditto	96
Louis Desforges	Ditto	96
Hastings Hadley	Ditto	96
James Johnston	Ditto	48
James Jackson	Ditto	48
George Lucas	Corporal	96
John Noble	First Lieutenant	102
John Roberts	Private	96
William Richardson	Ditto	48
John Q. Talbot	Ditto	48
William R. Willis	First lieutenant	204
Alexander A. White	Major	150

Making 15 for Louisiana.

23

A.—Continued.

LIST of Invalid Pensioners U. States, belonging to the state of Indiana, and payable at Vernon, Indiana, with the annual allowance to each annexed, viz:

		per annum.
George Antis	Private -	At $48
Thomas Almon	Ditto -	48
Robert Baird	Lieutenant -	136
Joseph Bartholomew	Lieutenant Colonel	270
John V. Buskirk	Private	96
Gaydon Branham	Ditto	72
Henry Bateman	Ditto	96
Robert Briggs	Ditto	48
Mathew Byrns	Ditto	48
Godfrey Hall Balding	Sergeant	96
Hugh Barns	Chaplain	240
William Crist	Private	48
William Collins	Ditto	48
Samuel Little	Second Lieutenant	180
Zachariah Lindley	Sergeant -	48

A.—Continued.

		per annum.
Peter M'Mickle	Private	At £48
Daniel Minor	Ditto	96
John Norris	Captain	120
Samuel Potter	Private	96
Adam Stropes	Ditto	96
Silas Siansbury	Musician	96
William Samuels	Private	82
Joseph Wasson	Ditto	96
Humphry Webster	First lieutenant	240
William B. Welsh	Sergeant	84

Making 25 Invalid Pensioners for Indiana.

A.—Continued.

LIST of Invalid Pensioners of the U. States, for the state of Mississippi, paid at Fort St. Stephen's, with the annual allowance to each annexed, viz:

			per annum.
John Booth	. . .	Sergeant major .	At $72
Charles Forrister	. . .	Private .	96
John S. Hackett	. . .	Third Lieutenant	168
Robert J. Lowry	. . .	First lieutenant	51
Henry Morris, jun.	. . .	Private .	64
Ebenezer Smith	. . .	Ditto . .	48
David Welsh, or Welch	. . .	Ditto. . .	96

Making 7 Invalid Pensioners for Mississippi.

A.—Continued.

LIST of U. States Invalid Pensioners for the Missouri Territory, paid at St. Louis, with the annual allowance to each annexed, viz:

		At $76 80 per annum.
Isaac Burnham	Private	
Michael Chapu	Ditto	48
Stephen Hempstead	Ditto	72
Joseph Henderson	Lieutenant	102
Benjamin Haile	Private	48
Nathan Heald	Major	240
Daniel Kenny	Private	96
Joshua Miller	Captain	96
Cristopher Mourning	Private	57 60
Andrew S. M‘Girk	Ditto	72
John Patterson	Ditto	48
Thomas Stokely	Ditto	2¾
George Thompson	Ditto	96

Making 13 Invalid Pensioners for Missouri Territory.

A.—Continued.

LIST of U. States Invalid Pensioners for Michigan Territory, paid at Detroit, with the annual allowance to each annexed, viz:

					At $72 per annum.
George Best	Private	. . . .	. . . .	. . . .	At $72
Richard Bean	Ditto	. . . .	. . . .	. . . .	72
John Heaton	Ditto	. . . .	. . . .	. . . .	53 68
William Letts	Ditto	. . . .	. . . .	. . . .	38 40
John Luther	Ditto	. . . .	. . . .	. . . .	64
Miles S. Miller	Ditto	. . . .	. . . .	. . . .	96
John Reynolds	Ditto	. . . .	. . . .	. . . .	57 60

Making 7 Invalid Pensioners for Michigan.

A.—Continued.

LIST of U. States Invalid Pensioners for the Illinois Territory, paid at Kaskaskia, with the annual allowance to each annexed, viz:

		At $96 per annum.
Julian Bart	Private	96
Samuel Jackaway	Ditto	48
John Myers	Ditto	64
William Pruitt	Ditto	96
Charles Revere	Ditto	96
George Saunders	Ditto	96
Thomas Williams	Ditto	96

Making 7 Invalid Pensioners for Illinois.

A.—Continued.

LIST of United States' Invalid Pensioners for the District of Columbia, paid at Washington City, with the annual allowance to each annexed, viz.

			per annum.
John Archdeacon	Private		At $32
William Bond	Ditto		96
John Butler	Ditto		96
Bayne S. Berry	Ditto		64
Alexander Barrett	Ditto		32
James D. Brown	Second lieutenant		180
Samuel Barnes	Private		48
George Bamover	Ditto		96
Samuel Y. Balch	Second lieutenant		180
Henry Carberry	Captain		240
John Calhoun	Private		48
John Carv	Ditto		32
Richard Calligan	Corporal		72
Henry Creegan	Private		96
Louis Desnoyers	Ditto		48
Francis Dubois	Ditto		32

A.—Continued.

Name	Rank	At $48 per annum.
Walter Dyer	Private	48
James Evans	Ditto	96
Robert Evans	Ditto	72
Daniel Eginton	Ditto	48
John Ent	Corporal	48
George G Gretton	Private	31 92
William Hamilton	Ditto	24
Charles Kelly	Ditto	48
Ambrose Lewis	Ditto	72
John B. Labranche	Ditto	48
Samuel Lane	Major	300
Henly M'Farland	Private	38 40
James Murphy	Ditto	32
William R M'Kay	Sergeant	48
Philip Markley	Private	48
Peter Mills	Captain	48
Michael M'Dermott	Private	48
Charles Neil	Ditto	76 80
Richard Osborn	Ditto	48
John Pierre or Piars	Musician	96
James Perry	Private	96

A.—Continued.

		per annum.
Thomas Pendel	Sergeant major	At $96
Maurice Pearce	Private	48
Robert Piper	Ditto	72
Samuel Russ	Ditto	48
Hugh Robb	Ditto	48
Antoine Razé	Musician	32
John Rauth	Private	48
Thomas Simmons	Ditto	96
Edmund Stevenson	Ditto	96
Clement Sewall	Ensign	12½ 80
Titus V. Sliter	Private	48
James Scott	Ditto	96
John Welch	Ditto	64

Making 50 invalid pensioners for the District of Columbia.

WAR DEPARTMENT, PENSION OFFICE, March 5th, 1818.

GEORGE BOYD.

Hon. J. C. Calhoun, Secretary of War.

A.—Continued.

LIST *of half-pay pensioners of the United States, arising from relinquishments of bounty land, belonging to the state of New Hampshire, and paid at Portsmouth, with the annual allowance annexed to each, viz:*

		Per annum.
Elizabeth Piper	Guardian of the heirs of Jonathan Piper,	Private	$48
Noah Bisbee	Ditto	Noah Bisbee, jun.	Sergeant	48
Benjamin B. Darling	Ditto	Ebenezer Truston	Private	48
Mary Henderson	Ditto	John Henderson	Ditto	48
Benjamin Davis	Ditto	Dummer Pattee	Ditto	48
John Grant	Ditto	James Sergeant	Ditto	48
Darius D. Evans	Ditto	Thomas Pool	Ditto	48
Abrose Gold	Ditto	Isaac Lawrence	Ditto	48
John Shipley	Ditto	William Lovejoy	Ditto	48
Levi George	Ditto	Moses Bailey	Ditto	48
John Montgomery	Ditto	Jonathan Ring	Ditto	48
Timothy Richardson	Ditto	Benjamin Goodwin	Ditto	48
John Root	Ditto	Henry Eastman	Sergeant	66
Sarah Littlefield	Ditto	George Littlefield	Private	48
Jonathan Crawford	Ditto	Robert Crawford	Ditto	48
John Bennett	Ditto	John A. H. Jackson	Ditto	48
Nathaniel Souther	Ditto	Thomas Chandler	Corporal	60
Mary Shorey	Ditto	Daniel Shorey	Private	48
Simon Johnson	Ditto	Thomas Dearborn	Corporal	60

A.—Continued.

			Per annum.
Andrew Demerritt	Guardian of the heirs of Samuel T. Emerson	Private	48
Mehitabel Kelly	Ditto Joseph Kelly	Ditto	48
Benjamin B. Darling	Ditto Abel Kimball	Ditto	48
Peter Whitter	Ditto Samuel Tollinsbee	Ditto	48
Darius D. Evans	Ditto Samuel Moores	Ditto	48
Darius B. Evans	Ditto Jonathan Simonds	Ditto	48
Betsy Tandy	Ditto William Tandy	Ditto	48
Sarah Bigelow	Ditto Elnathan Bigelow	Ditto	48
William Morrill	Ditto Thomas Fisher	Ditto	48
James Roberts	Ditto Tristram Goodwin	Ditto	48
John Chick	Ditto George Abbott	Ditto	48
John Folsom	Ditto John Melvin	Ditto	48
John Bowman	Ditto Henry Goodenough	Ditto	48
Daniel Gale, 3d.	Ditto Richard Moulton	Ditto	48
Jesse Blake	Ditto William Evans	Ditto	48
Horatio G. Prescott	Ditto Francis Bowman	Ditto	48

Making 35 for New Hampshire.

A.—Continued.

LIST of half-pay pensioners of the United States, arising from relinquishments of bounty land, belonging to the state of Massachusetts, and paid at Boston, with the annual allowance annexed to each, viz.

			Per annum.
Lydia Moody	Guardian of the heirs of John S. Moody	Corporal	$ 60
David Quimby	Ditto	Patrick Dorsey	Private	48
John Reed	Ditto	Jonathan Clark	Ditto	48
Betsey Freeman	Ditto	Scott Freeman	Ditto	48
Bathsheba Vickery	Ditto	Elijah Vickery	Ditto	48
Sophia Haraden	Ditto	Elisha Haraden	Ditto	48
Jacob Metcalf	Ditto	Nathaniel Walker	Corporal	60
Solomon Warner	Ditto	Joseph Staples	Private	48
Elisha Briggs	Ditto	Daniel Smith	Ditto	48
Prudence Fay	Ditto	Benjamin Ward	Ditto	48
Elza Chadwick	Ditto	Benjamin Chadwick	Ditto	48
Thomas Foster	Ditto	Elisha Goodnow	Ditto	48
Timothy L. Jennison	Ditto	Luke Pool	Sergeant	66
William Sizer	Ditto	Darius Truesdale	Private	48
Andrew Knowlton	Ditto	Samuel Rice	Ditto	48
Andrew Blake	Ditto	James Macumber	Corporal	60

A.—Continued.

Name		Rank	Per annum.
Andrew Knowlton	Guardian of the heirs of James Morton	Private	$48
Mary Oldes	Ditto	John Oldes	Ditto	48
Elijah Hatch	Ditto	Simeon Jones	Corporal	60
Catherine Dalrymple	Ditto	Henry Dalrymple	Sergeant	66
Willis Patten	Ditto	Isaac Whittier	Ditto	66
Betsy Lessley	Ditto	Samuel Lessley	Ditto	66
Betsy Trafford	Ditto	George Trafford	Private	48
Esther Reed	Ditto	Moses Reed	Ditto	48
Christiana Eastburn	Ditto	John Eastburn	Ditto	48
Ichabod Leonard	Ditto	Stephen Smith	Musician	54
George Osgood	Ditto	Nathan Smith	Private	48
Samuel Hutchins	Ditto	John Ham	Ditto	48
Nabby Newcomb	Ditto	Oliver Newcomb	Sergeant	66
Marcy Smith	Ditto	Robert Smith	Private	48
John Smith	Ditto	Perry Lawton	Ditto	48
Sally Crossman	Ditto	Seth Crossman	Ditto	48
Sally Billings	Ditto	Benjamin Billings	Ditto	48
Susanna Glover	Ditto	Joshua Glover	Ditto	48
Ruth Bowen	Ditto	Amos Bowen	Ditto	48
Molly Kelton	Ditto	James Kelton	Ditto	48
Samuel F. Cutler and Chirity Dexter }	Ditto	Eleazer Dexter	Ditto	48

A.—Continued.

			Per annum.
Ruth Morrill -	Guardian of the heirs of Enoch Merrill	Private	$ 48
Elizabeth Whiston	Ditto Francis Whiston	Ditto	48
Hopeful Allen -	Ditto Noah Allen	Corporal	60
James M'Kinstrey -	Ditto Amasa Woodward	Private	48
Ebenezer C. Richardson	Ditto Dr. William Ramsdale	Ditto	48

Making 42 for Massachusetts.

A.—Continued.

LIST of half-pay Pensioners of the United States, arising from relinquishments of land, belonging to the state of Connecticut, and paid at Middletown, with the annual allowance annexed to each, viz:

			Per annum.
John Landon	Guardian of the heirs of John Landon, jun.	Corporal	$ 60
B‹ts› Paine	Ditto	Private	48
Otis Robinson	Ditto	Ditto	48
Priscilla Arnold	Ditto	Ditto	48
Enos Hopkins	Ditto	Corporal	60
John G. Allen	Ditto	Private	48
Asa Ward	Ditto	Ditto	48
Catharine Dennison	Ditto	Ditto	48
Lucy Lebar	Ditto	Sergeant	66
John Andrews	Ditto	Private	48
Sophia Armstrong	Ditto	Di:to	48
Rebecca Richmond	Ditto	Ditte	48

The names with relinquishments:

David Paine	Lyman Perkins	Benedict Arnold
Henry Levi	David O. Allen	Orange Smith
Joseph Dennison	Jacob Lebar	Thomas Janes
Dyer Armstrong	Anthony Richmond	

Making 12 for Connecticut.

A.—Continued.

LIST of half pay Pensioners of the United States, arising from relinquishments of bounty land, belonging to the state of Vermont, and paid at Bennington, with the annual allowance annexed to each, viz.

			Per annum.
Asa Aikins	Guardian of the heirs of Ralph Howard	Private	$ 48
Patty Bishop	Eleazer Bishop	Corporal	60
Ebenezer Adams	Luther Adams	Private	48
David G. Perkins	John Perkins, jr.	Musician	54
Nathaniel Whitcomb	Rufus Tenant	Private	48
Rachael Coburn	Jonathan Coburn	Ditto	48
Benjamin Demmon	Robert Miller	Ditto	48
Mary Cook	James T. Cook	Ditto	48
Levi Lamb	Samuel Stephens	Ditto	48
Amy Messenger	William S. Messender	Ditto	48
Hannah Sealy and Sylvanus Damford	Reuben Segent	Ditto	48
Elijah Allen	Benjamin Rogers	Corporal	60
Nathaniel Hall	James Bassford	Private	48
Marcy Hoyt	Daniel H Hoyt	Ditto	48
Electa Prior	Hubble S. Fuller	Corporal	60

25

A.—Continued.

Name		Rank	Per annum.
William Deanison	Guardian of the heirs of Artemas Taft	Private	$ 48
Martha Jordan	Jeremiah Jordan	Ditto	48
Sarah Silver	David Silver	Ditto	48
Sally Liscum	Peletiah D. Liscum	Sergeant	66
Rebecca Stewart	John Stewart	Private	48
John Griswold, jun.	Lufkin Heath	Ditto	48
William Strong	John Collins	Ditto	48
Joseph Clark	Elizur Simonds	Ditto	48
Lucy Kilham	John Killam	Ditto	48
Betsy Wilcox	Nathaniel Wilcox	Ditto	48
Hannah Pingree	James Pingree	Ditto	48
Oliver Booge	Alexander M'Arthur	Ditto	48
Oliver Phillips	Joshua Phillips	Ditto	48
Asahel Langworthy	Seth S. Robbins	Ditto	48
Orlin Bostwick	Elijah Branch	Ditto	48
Phebe Daniels	Samuel Daniels	Ditto	48
Daniel Martin	Rufus I. Lillie	Sergeant	66
William Barber	William P. Morey	Private	48
Sabra Mighell	John W. Mighell	Ditto	48
Jeremiah Nelson	Abel Sanderson	Ditto	48
Rebecca Griswold	Elisha Griswold	Ditto	48
Joel H. Linsley	Harry Smith	Sergeant	66

Making 87 for Vermont.

A.—Continued.

LIST of half-pay*Pensioners of the United States, arising from relinquishments of bounty land, belonging to the state of New York, and paid at the city of New York, with the annual allowance annexed to each, viz.

			Per annum.
Sally Burnett	Guardian of the heirs of Samuel Burnett	Private	$ 48
Mary Van Riper	Ditto Isaac Van Riper	Ditto	48
Ann M'Mullen	Ditto George Freeland, alias Hugh M'Mullen		
Mary Force	Ditto Baldwin Force	Ditto	48
Abraham Lent	Ditto Albert Van Tassel	Ditto	48
Catharine Stewart	Ditto Abraham Stewart	Ditto	48
Maria Stevens	Ditto William Stevens	Sergeant	66
Catharine Hicks	Ditto Thomas Hicks	Private	48
Rachel Lawrence	Ditto Thomas Lawrence	Ditto	48
Lydia Francisco	Ditto Israel Francisco	Ditto	48
Sarah Allen	Ditto Andrew Allen	Ditto	48
Catharine Keen	Ditto Henry R. Keen	Ditto	48
Nancy Minton	Ditto Nathan Minton	Ditto	48
Hannah Whitehead	Ditto Mahlon Whitehead	Corporal	60
Naomi S Lester	Ditto Bennett Lester	Private	48
Reuben Cogswell	Ditto Milton Bowers	Sergeant	66

B.—Continued.

Name	Guardian	Relationship	Rank	Per annum.
Clarissa Foreman	Robert Foreman.	Guardian of the heirs of	Private	$48
James Pettit	Abraham Stagg	Ditto	Ditto	48
Ann Gordon	Isaac Gordon	Ditto	Ditto	48
Hannah Carter	William Carter	Ditto	Ditto	48
Weltel Willoughby	Lewis Baker	Ditto	Ditto	48
Nathan Wheeler	Job Harris	Ditto	Ditto	48
Hannah Lindsley	Jonathan Lindsley	Ditto	Ditte	48
Abigail Jones	Amos Jones	Ditto	Ditto	48
Jane Watters	Samuel Watters	Ditto	Ditto	48
Hannah Courter	James Courter	Ditto	Ditto	48
Sarah Wandell	Alexander Wandell	Ditto	Ditto	48
Charlotte Hunter	Joel Hunter	Ditto	Ditto	48
Cornelius Schuyler	John Annely	Ditto	Ditto	48
Ann Thompson	Benj. C. Thompson	Ditto	Corporal	60
Mary Ennis	Sylvanus Ennis	Ditto	Private	48
Joanna Johnson	David Johnson	Ditto	Ditto	48
Hannah Woodward	Israel Woodward	Ditto	Ditto	48
Sarah Williams	Isaac Williams	Ditto	Ditto	48
Prudence Ford	Thomas Hunt	Ditto.	Sergeant	48
Polly Lincoln	Perez Lincoln	Ditto	Private	48
Henry Reynolds	Benjamin Lawrence	Ditto.	Corporal	60.

A.—Continued.

			Per annum.
Nancy Griswold	Guardian of the heirs of Josiah Griswold	Private	$ 48
Hannah Willis	Ditto	William Willis	Ditto	48
Martha Curry	Ditto	Thomas Curry	Ditto	48
Sarah Bates	Ditto	Joseph Bates	Ditto	48
Wealthy Roberts	Ditto	Samuel Roberts	Ditto	48
Elizabeth Spencer	Ditto	Jasper G. Spencer	Ditto	48
Eve Grant	Ditto	Godfrey Grant	Ditto	48
William Pitt Platt	Ditto	Francis Miller	Ditto	48
Ellis M'Donald	Ditto	Elisha M'Donald	Ditto	48
Laura Edmonds	Ditto	Robert Edmonds	Ditto	48
Richard Lacy	Ditto	Nicholas Vanloon	Ditto	48
Elizabeth Schofield	Ditto	William Schofield	Ditto	48
Joseph Waterbury	Ditto	Joseph Schofield	Ditto	48
Sarah Beach	Ditto	Samuel Beach	Ditto	48
Martin S. Waller	Ditto	Thomas Jones	Ditto	48
Betsy Knowlton	Ditto	Joshua Knowlton	Ditto	48
Phebe Crawford	Ditto	Absalom Crawford	Ditto	48
Sarah Weed	Ditto	John Weed	Ditto	48
Molly Dumbolton	Ditto	Benjamin Dumbolton alias Dumbleton	Ditto	48
John Aikley	Ditto.	Robert Britt	Ditto	48

A.—Continued.

			Per annum.
Eleanor McIntosh	Guardian of the heirs of James McIntosh	Private	$48
Diana Brooks	Ditto	John Brooks	Ditto	48
Susanna Flynn	Ditto	Peter Flynn	Ditto	48
Mary Parrott	Ditto	Abraham Parrott	Ditto	48
John Shark	Ditto	Gershom Northrop	Ditto	48
Moses Olmstead	Ditto	John Franklin	Ditto	48
Albert C. Hall	Ditto	Caleb Babcock	Ditto	48
Lucy Stephenson	Ditto	Thomas Stephenson	Ditto	48
Thomas Hall	Ditto	Hezekiah Hubbard	Ditto	48
Arena Steeds	Ditto	John Steeds	Sergeant	66
James D. Bemis	Ditto	Daniel Ward	Private	48
Elizabeth Allen	Ditto	John Allen, 2d	Ditto	48
Ebenezer Reed	Ditto	George Bradley	Ditto	48
Jedediah Smith	Ditto	Jesse Arnold	Ditto	48

Making 71 for New York.

A.—Continued.

LIST of half-pay Pensioners of the United States, arising from relinquishments of bounty land, belonging to the state of New Jersey, and paid at Trenton, with the annual allowance annexed to each, viz:

		Per annum.
Henry Brevoort	Guardian of the heirs of John Brevoort	Private	$ 48
Alexander Kirkpatrick	Ditto Moses Roff	Ditto	48
Jacob Terheun	Ditto Albert Terheun	Ditto	48
Arthur Powell	Ditto Joseph Powell	Ditto	48
Hannah-Brinnesholtz and } Joseph Woodruff }	Ditto Henry Brinnesholtz	{ Ditto Ditto	48 48
Hannah Mattson	Ditto John Mattson	Ditto	48
Nancy Robinson	Ditto William Robinson	Ditto	48
Sasannah Ireland	Ditto Ezekiel Ireland	Ditto	48
Levi Price	Ditto Robert Nelson	Ditto	48
Betsy Brown	Ditto Aaron Brown	Ditto	48
William J. Bowne	Ditto Cornelius Larney	Ditto	48

Makin 11 for New Jersey.

A—Continued.

LIST of half-pay Pensioners of the United States, arising from relinquishments of bounty land, belonging to the state of Pennsylvania, and paid at Philadelphia, with the annual allowance annexed to each, viz:

			Per annum.
Susannah Coyle	Guardian of the heirs of William Coyle alias Coil	Private	$ 48
Benjamin Pearson	Ditto	Ditto	48
Mary Totterson	Ditto	Ditto	48
John M'Clelland	Ditto	Ditto	48
Stephen Crane	Ditto	Ditto	48
John Bell	Ditto	Ditto	48
Abraham Humberd	Ditto	Ditto	48
Alexander Johnston	Ditto	Ditto	48
John Hadden	Ditto	Ditto	48
John Withrow	Ditto	Ditto	48
Samuel Jackson	Ditto	Ditto	48
Esther Hemphill	Ditto	Ditto	48
Ann Derickson	Ditto	Sergeant	66
John L. Pearson	Ditto	Private	48
Elizabeth Boss	Ditto	Ditto	48

Column contents (names listed with corresponding claimant)
William Coyle alias Coil
Joshua Ash
Henry Totterson
James M. Barber
Josiah Moore
James Hall
Sam'l Rickey or Richey
George White
Freeman Wheaton
James Williams
James Jones
Samuel Hemphill
Joseph Derrickson
William Price
Garret Boss

A.—Continued.

			Per annum.
26 Elizabeth Angel	Guardian of the heirs of Michael Angel	Private	$48
Sarah Miller	Ditto	Ditto	48
Samuel Smith	Ditto	Ditto	48
Samuel Smith	Ditto	Ditto	48
Jacob Gantz	Ditto	Ditto	48
Thomas M'Kennan	Ditto	Ditto	48
George Kauffett	Ditto	Ditto	48
Andrew Dunlap and Isabella M'Annelly }	Ditto	Ditto	48
William Smilie	Ditto	Sergeant	66
Maria Carr	Ditto	Ditto	48
Sarah Allen	Ditto	Private	48
Susannah King	Ditto	Ditto	48
Charles Dowd	Ditto	Ditto	48
F'lisha Lister	Ditto	Ditto	48
Elizabeth Huber	Ditto	Ditto	48
Benjamin Hellen	Ditto	Ditto	48
Catherine Ord	Ditto	Ditto	48
John M'Clelland	Ditto	Ditto	48
Catharine Orr	Ditto	Ditto	48
Ann Ashby	Ditto	Ditto	48

A.—Continued.

			Per annum.
Thomas Maxwell - -	Guardian of the heirs of William F. Maxwell	Private	$48
Catherine Kruson -	Ditto Jacob Kruson	Ditto	48
Samuel Bramin -	Ditto Benjamin Bramin	Ditto	48
Robert Darrah and Ann } Dickey -	Ditto John Dickey	Ditto	48
Fridget Ferry -	Ditto Dennis Ferry	Ditto	48
John Holmes	Ditto John W. Sickles	Ditto	48

Making 41 for Pennsylvania.

A.—Continued.

LIST *of the half-pay Pensioner of the United States, arising from relinquishment of bounty land, belonging to the state of Delaware, and paid at New Castle, with the annual allowance annexed to him, viz.*

| John Dixon | Guardian of the heirs of William Robinson | Private | $ 48 per annum. |

LIST *of half-pay Pensioners of the United States, arising from relinquishments of bounty land, belonging to the state of Maryland, and paid at Baltimore, with the annual allowance annexed to each, viz.*

			Per annum.
Elizabeth Boran	Guardian of the heirs of John Boran	Private	$ 48
Ann Cornelius	Ditto	Ditto	48
George Crandell	Ditto	Ditto	48
Bridget Byrnes	John Burns or Byrnes	Ditto	48
Mary Ross	David Ross	Ditto	48
Eleanor Hannah	William Hannah	Ditto	48

A.—Continued.

		Per annum.
Susanna Livers	Guardian of the heirs of John Livers	$ 48
Mary Fish	Ditto Levin Fish	48
Mary Grapevine	Ditto Frederick Grapevine	48
Mary Yohn	Ditto John Yohn	48
Elizabeth Rictor	Ditto Christian Rictor	48
Daniel W. Norris	Ditto Michael Kelly	48

Making 12 for Maryland.

A.—Continued.

LIST of half-pay Pensioners of the United States, arising from relinquishments of bounty land, belonging to the state of Virginia, and paid at Richmond, with the annual allowances annexed to each, viz.

			Per annum.
William R. Chapman	Guardian of the heirs of Thomas M. Money	Private	$ 48
Rebecca Brewer	Ditto	Zachariah Brewer	Corporal	60
James Newell	Ditto	Jonathan Bell	Private	48
Henry W. Wills	Ditto	Henry Morris	Ditto	48
Elizabeth Reynolds	Ditto	John Reynolds	Ditto	48
Anr. Hardy	Ditto	John Hardy	Corporal	60
James Jack	Ditto	David Love	Private	48
Rachael Clark	Ditto	John Mills	Ditto	48
Samuel Patterson	Ditto	John Porter	Ditto	48
Jane Robinson	Ditto	Archibald Robinson	Ditto	48
Lemuel Thompson	Ditto	Valentine Ingram	Ditto	48

Making 11 for Virginia.

A.—Continued.

LIST of half-pay Pensioners of the United States, arising from relinquishments of bounty land, belonging to the state of South Carolina, and paid at Charleston, with the annual allowance annexed to each, viz:

			Per annum.
Janes Coleman	Guardian of the heirs of Noah Coleman	Private	$ 48
Elizabeth Pointer	Ditto Thomas Pointer	Ditto	48
Mary Cunningham	Ditto John Cunningham	Ditto	48

Making 3 for South Carolina.

A.—Continued.

LIST of half-pay Pensioners of the United States, arising from relinquishments of bounty land, belonging to the state of Kentucky, and paid at Lexington, with the annual allowance annexed to each, viz.

			Per annum.
John Wade	Guardian of the heirs of Henry Brown	Private	$ 48
Levikia Goans	Ditto	James Guines or Goans	Ditto	48
Henry R. Graham	Ditto	Richard Tible	Ditto	48
Sally Redding	Ditto	William Redding	Ditto	48
John Hughes	Ditto	Hugh Scott	Ditto	48
Daniel M'C. Paines	Ditto	Robert Reed	Ditto	48
Daniel M'C. Paine	Ditto	Beverly A. Blake	Ditto	48
Henry Scott	Ditto	David Scott	Ditto	48
Janes Gaines	Ditto	Thomas Gaines	Ditto	48
Daniel M'Carty Paine	Ditto	Nathaniel Robinson	Ditto	48
Daniel M'C. Paine	Ditto	Braxton Blake	Ditto	48

Making 11 for Kentucky.

A.—Continued.

LIST *of half-pay Pensioners of the United States, arising from relinquishments of bounty land, belonging to the state of Tennessee, and paid at Nashville, with the annual allowance annexed to each, viz.*

		Per annum.
Sarah Tankersly	Guardian of the heirs of William Tankersly	Private	$ 48
Jane Waddle	Ditto Jacob Waddle	Ditto	48
Mary Dyer	Ditto Baldy Dyer	Ditto	48
Mary Connor	Ditto Isaac Connor	Ditto	48

Making 4 for Tennessee.

A.—Continued.

LIST of half-pay Pensioners of the United States, arising from relinquishments of bounty land, belonging to the state of Ohio, and paid at Chillicothe, with the annual allowance annexed to each, viz:

			Per annum.
Anthony Ritzer	Guardian of the heirs of Stephen Hallman	Private	$48
Rosanna Rice	Ditto	John Rice	Ditto	48
Naomi Timmons	Ditto	Eli Timmons	Ditto	48
Amos Harris	Ditto	Samuel Everhart	Ditto	48
George Foglesong	Ditto	William March	Ditto	48
John Marks	Ditto	Zachariah North	Corporal	60
Robert Taylor	Ditto	Robert Oliver	Private	48
David Jennings	Ditto	Henry Fryman	Ditto	48
Samuel Hearn	Ditto	Joseph Dodds	Ditto	48
Peter Grubb	Ditto	Jacob W. Davis	Sergeant	66
Henry H. Evans	Ditto	William Landsdown	Private	48
Nicholas Davis	Ditto	Robert Morrison	Ditto	48
Moses Crist	Ditto	Hugh Gaston	Ditto	48

Making 13 for Ohio.

27

A.—Continued.

LIST of half-pay Pensioners of the United States, arising from relinquishments of bounty land, belonging to the District of Maine, and paid at Portland, with the annual allowance annexed to each, viz.

			Per annum.
William Tuttle	Guardian of the heirs of Josiah Smith	Corporal	$ 60
John Bean	Ditto Joseph Levett	Private	48
Peter York	Ditto Ezekiel Duston	Ditto	48
Aaron Chamberlin	Ditto Nathaniel Stearns	Ditto	48
Charles Gowell	Ditto Solomon Messervey	Ditto	48
Abigail Hall	Ditto Daniel Hall	Artificer	78
Jeremiah Bradbury	Ditto Jonathan Sergeant	Private	48
Jeremiah Bradbury	Ditto Joseph Bridges	Ditto	48
Ephraim Stinchfield	Ditto Benjamin Clarke	Ditto	48
Abigail Dunbar	Ditto Samuel Dunbar	Ditto	48
Caleb Bradley	Ditto Joseph Noyes	Ditto	48
Rachael Saunders	Ditto Nathan Saunders	Ditto	48
Charles Hall	Ditto William Tufts	Sergeant	48
Charles Hall	Ditto Robert Rogers	Ditto	66
Eunice Russell	Ditto Benjamin Russell	Private	48
Oakes Perry	Ditto Jonathan Philbrook	Ditto	48
Mary Chamberlain	Ditto Samuel Chamberlain	Ditto	48

A.—Continued.

Name	Relation	Heir	Rank	Per annum.
James W. Ripley	Guardian of the heirs of	Samuel Carpenter	Private	$48
Lois Evans	Ditto	Robert Evans	Corporal	60
Elizabeth Mann	Ditto	Daniel Mann	Sergeant	66
John Simontown	Ditto	Charles Coburn	Ditto	66
Joel R. Ellis	Ditto	William Haskell	Private	48
Nathan Lord	Ditto	Jacob Lord	Ditto	48
Elizabeth Hussey	Ditto	Zachariah Hussey	Ditto	48
Anstreus Chapham	Ditto	Stephen Chapham	Ditto	48
Catharine Harlow	Ditto	Jabez Harlow	Sergeant	66
Robert C. Vose	Ditto	John Springer	Ditto	66
Reuben Bean	Ditto	Levi Eldridge	Private	48
William Emmons	Ditto	Daniel Horn	Ditto	48
Moses Michaels	Ditto	Ezra Cole	Ditto	48
Susanna Dorsett	Ditto	Jedediah Dorsett	Ditto	48
James Marston	Ditto	James Douglass	Ditto	48
Eusebius Weston	Ditto	Amos Baker	Ditto	48
Hannah Glidden	Ditto	Winthrop Glidden	Ditto	48
John Hovey	Ditto	John Gold	Ditto	48
Pitt Dillingham	Ditto	Eleazer Cummings	Ditto	48
Gideon Wing	Ditto	Asa Wing	Ditto	48
Jones Shaw	Ditto	Joseph Witham	Ditto	48

A.—Continued.

			Per annum.
Mary Moore	Guardian of the heirs of John Moore	Private	$ 48
Isaac Bragg	Bolton Fish	Sergeant	66
Nicholas Davis, jun.	Ditto Dearborn T. Blake	Private	48
Benjamin Bourne, jun.	Ditto John Haines	Ditto	48
Peasely Morrill, jun.	Ditto James Le Baron	Ditto	48
James Young	Ditto William Mitchell	Ditto	48
Brown Baker	Ditto Joseph Littlefield	Ditto	48
Enoch Noyes	Ditto Thomas Eustis	Drummer	54
Josiah Newman	Ditto John M'Laughlin	Private	48
Martha Clark	Ditto Joseph Clark	Ditto	48
Hezekiah Frost	Ditto Benjamin Rowe	Ditto	48
Moses Moody	Ditto John Bolden	Ditto	48
David Miller	Ditto Samuel Boynton	Ditto	48

Making 51 for the District of Maine.

LIST *of the half pay Pensioner of the United States, arising from relinquishment of bounty land, belonging to the Illinois Territory, and paid at Kaskaskia, with the annual allowance annexed to her, viz:*

			Per annum.
Patsey Clark	Guardian of the heirs of Thomas F. Clark	Private.	$ 48

A.—Continued.

LIST of half-pay Pensioners of the United States, arising from relinquishments of bounty land, belonging to the District of Columbia, with the annual allowance annexed to each, viz:

				Per annum.
Sarah Robertson	Guardian of the heirs of Joseph Robertson		Corporal	$60
Ammi Kelton	Ditto	James F. Musingo	Private	48
Susan Bentley	Ditto	Jonas Bentley	Ditto	48
Mary Burch	Ditto	Theophilus Y. Burch	Ditto	48
Catharine Medcalf	Ditto	John D. Medcalf	Ditto	48
Edward Ford	Ditto	John B. Dyer	Ditto	48
Elizabeth Hughes	Ditto	Zachariah Hughes	Ditto	48
Mary Leech	Ditto	Samuel Leech	Ditto	48
Rebecca Tuell	Ditto	Roderick Tuell	Ditto	60
Richard Sheckels	Ditto	Jacob Potts	Artificer	48
Hepsey Swallow	Ditto	Zephaniah Swallow	Private	48
Susanna Jackson	Ditto	George Jackson	Ditto	48
Samuel Wheeler	Ditto	Sinclair Carroll	Ditto	48
Alice Collins	Ditto	John Collins	Ditto	48

Making 14 for the District of Columbia.

WAR DEPARTMENT,
PENSION BUREAU, March 7th, 1848.

GEORGE BOYD.

Hon. J. C. Calhoun, Secretary of War.

RECAPITULATION, viz:

		Pensioners.
New Hampshire - - - -	Invalid	164
	Half-pay	35
Massachusetts - - - -	Invalid	418
	Half-pay	42
District of Maine - - - -	Invalid	36
	Half-pay	51
Connecticut - - - -	Invalid	200
	Half-pay	12
Rhode Island - - - -	Invalid	31
Vermont - - - - -	Invalid	161
	Half-pay	37
New York - - - - -	Invalid	905
	Half-pay	71
New Jersey - - - - -	Invalid	57
	Half-pay	11
Pennsylvania - - - - -	Invalid	406
	Half-pay	41
Delaware - - - - -	Invalid	21
	Half-pay	1
Maryland - - - - -	Invalid	269
	Half-pay	12
Virginia - - - - -	Invalid	240
	Half pay	11
North Carolina - - - -	Invalid	87
South Carolina - - - - -	Invalid	22
	Half-pay	3
Georgia - - - - -	Invalid	26
Kentucky - - - - -	Invalid	94
	Half-pay	11
Tennessee - - - - -	Invalid	84
	Half-pay	4
Ohio - - - - -	Invalid	99
	Half-pay	13
Louisiana - - - - -	Invalid	15
Indiana - - - - -	Invalid	25
Mississippi - - - -	Invalid	7
Missouri Territory - - -	Invalid	13
Michigan Territory - - -	Invalid	7
Illinois Territory - - - -	Invalid	7
	Half-pay	1
District of Columbia - - - -	Invalid	50
	Half-pay	14
Total amount		**3,814**

B.

STATEMENT, showing the Widows and Orphans who are inscribed on the books of this office, as half-pay pensioners, for five years, conformably to the laws of the United States, especially the first section of the act of April the 16th, 1816, "the sum annually paid to each, and the states or territories in which the said pensioners are respectively paid," made in obedience to a resolution of the Senate of the United States, passed under date of February the 22d, 1818.

NEW HAMPSHIRE.

No.	Names of decedents, &c.	Rank or grade.	Original commencement of pension.	Pension per month.	Pension per annum.	Remarks, &c.
1	Brigham, Thomas, *widow*	Private	5th July, 1814	$4 00	$48 00	
2	Cogswell, Thos. *widow*	Do.	26th Oct. 1813	4	48	
3	Call, Silas, *widow*	Captain	8th Nov. 1814	20	240	
4	Glines, Benjamin, *widow*	Private	20th Dec. 1813	4	48	
5	Glover, Stephen, *widow*	Do.	8th Nov. 1813	4	48	
6	Gage, William, *widow*	Sergeant	17th April, 1813	5 50	66	
7	Howe, Amos, *widow*	Private	29th Sept. 1813	4	48	
8	Hoit, Paul J. *widow*	3d liutenant	5th Dec. 1814	11 50	138	
9	Hartford, John B. *widow*	Private	29th Sept. 1813	4	48	
10	Joy, Timothy M. *widow*	Do.	30th Nov. 1813	4	48	

B—Continued.

NEW HAMPSHIRE—Continued.

No.	Names of decedents, &c.	Rank or grade.	Original commencement of pension.	Pension per month.	Pension per annum.	Remarks, &c.
11	Moore, Jocob B. *widow*	Sugeon's mate	10th Jan. 1813	$15 00	$180 00	
12	Nute, William, *widow*	Private	1st Nov. 1813	4	48	
13	Nelson, John, *widow*	Do.	31st Aug. 1813	4	48	
14	Noble, Thomas, *widow*	Do.	14th Oct. 1813	4	48	
15	Pearl, Abraham, *widow*	Do.	25th Dec. 1813	4	48	
16	Perry, Nathan, *widow*	Do.	2d Nov. 1814	4	48	
17	Rand, Moses W. *widow*	Do.	26th Nov. 1813	4	48	
18	Shannon, William, *widow*	1st lieutenant	27th Aug. 1813	15	180	
19	Stephens, Theop. *widow*	Private	15th Oct. 1813	4	48	
20	Smith, Alpheus, *widow*	Do.	3d Nov. 1813	4	48	
21	Smith, Aaron, *widow*	Do.	5th Aug. 1813	4	48	
22	Tash, John, *widow*	Do.	21st Dec. 1813.	4	48	
23	Turrell, Abel, *widow*	Do.	7th Nov. 1813	4	48	
24	Tibbets, Peter, *widow*	Do.	21st Oct. 1813	4	48	
25	Wentworth, R. P. *widow*	Do.	16th Jan. 1814	4	48	
26	Wetherby, Daniel, *widow*	Do.	11th Jan. 1813	4	48	
					$1,812	

B—Continued.

DISTRICT OF MAINE.

No.	Names of decedents, &c.	Bank or grade.	Original commencement of pension.	Pension per month.	Pension per annum.	Remarks, &c.
27	Archibald, John, *widow*	Private	12th May, 1813	$4 00	$48 00	
28	Ames, Ezra, *widow*	Do.	1st Dec. 1814	4	48	
29	Bently, John, *widow*	Ensign	17th Sept. 1814	10	120	
30	Bean, Jonathan, *widow*	Private	26th Oct. 1813	4	48	
31	Bedell, Moses, *widow*	Do.	2d Dec. 1813	4	48	
32	Bridges, A. *wid. & children*	Do.	12th June, 1813	4	48	Widow died, February 11th, 1816.
33	Bryant, Ephraim, *widow.*	Do.	6th Nov. 1813	4	48	
34	Blye, James, *widow*	Do.	17th Aug. 1813	4	48	
35	Bangs, Benjamin, *widow*	Do.	12th May, 1813	4	48	
36	Center, Bernard, *widow*	Do.	18th Nov. 1813	4	48	
37	Cornish, Cyppreen, *widow*	Do.	29th April, 1813	4	48	
38	Chandler, Danl. R. *widow*	Corporal	3d Nov. 1813	5	60	
39	Cook, Nathaniel, *widow*	Private	25th April, 1813	4	48	
40	Dunham, Asa, *widow*	Do.	7th Oct. 1813	4	48	
41	Dutton, Boyal, *widow*	Do.	15th Sept. 1813	4	48	
42	Edgecomb, Gib. *widow*	Corporal	7th Jan. 1814	5	60	

B—Continued.

DISTRICT OF MAINE—Continued.

No.	Names of decedents, &c.	Rank or grade.	Original commencement of pension.	Pension per month.	Pension per annum.	Remarks, &c.
43	Fry, Samuel, *widow*	Private	14th May, 1813	$4 00	$48 00	
44	Fletcher, Gideon, *widow*	Do.	14th June - -	4	48	
45	Fowler, Royal, *widow*	Corporal	20th Nov. - -	5	60	
46	Freeman, Joseph, *child*	Private	30th May, -	4	48	
47	Cage, Stephen, *widow*	Do.	29th Jan. -	4	48	
48	Hardy, Thomas, *widow*	Do.	9th Dec. -	4	48	
49	Hutchens, Emery, *widow*	Do.	6th Nov. -	4	48	
50	Huzzey, John, *widow*	Do.	26th Oct. -	4	48	
51	Heirl, or Earl, Jacob, *widow and children*	Do.	4th May, -	4	48	Widow intermarried, 27th July, 1817.
52	Hancock, Stephen, *widow and child*	Do.	26th Dec. -	4	48	Widow intermarried, 18th Feb. 1816.
53	Hutchens, Simeon, *widow*	Do.	31st May, -	4	48	
54	Hustin, Noah, *widow*	Do.	25th Nov. -	4	48	
55	Hinckley, Russel, *widow*	Do.	6th May, -	4	48	
56	Johnson, Isaac, *widow*	Do.	1st Dec. -	4	48	

B—Continued.

DISTRICT OF MAINE—*Continued.*

No.	Names of decedents, &c.	Rank or grade.	Original commencement of pension.	Pension per month.	Pension per annum.	Remarks, &c.
57	Ingersoll Nathaniel, *widow and children*	Private	20th Dec. 1813	$4 00	$48 00	
58	Lumbard, Peter, *widow*	Do.	5th June, 1813	4	48	
59	Lord, William, *widow*	Do.	20th April, 1814	4	48	
60	Libby, Amos, *children*	Do.	26th Oct. 1813	4	48	
61	Leach, Nathan, *child*	Sergeant	16th May, -	5 50	66	
62	M'Llaughlin, Danl.*widow*	2d lieutenant	2d Nov. -	12 50	150	
63	M'Intire, James, *widow*	Private	24th Nov. -	4	48	
64	Nutter, Richard D.*widow*	Fifer	15th Nov. -	4 50	54	
65	Nash, William, *widow*	2d lieutenant	1st Oct. -	12 50	150	
66	Pool, Thomas, *widow and children*	Private	18th Jan. 1814	4	48	Widow intermarried, May 22d, 1815.
67	Procter, William, *widow and children*	Do.	1st Aug. -	4	48	Widow intermarried, June 15th, 1815.

B—Continued.

DISTRICT OF MAINE—*Continued.*

No	Names of decedents, &c.	Rank or grade.	Original commencement of pension.	Pension per month.	Pension per annum.	Remarks, &c.
68	Piper, Edward, *widow*	Private	11th May, 1813	$4	$48 00	
69	Rowe, Robert, *widow*	Do.	14th Nov. -	4	48	
70	Reed, Jones, *widow*	Do.	6th April, 1814	4	48	
71	Ricker, Nathaniel, *widow*	Do.	9th Nov. -	4	48	
72	Stacy, John, *widow*	Do.	27th Jan. -	4	48	
73	Smith, Jonathan, *widow*	Do.	29th March -	4	48	
74	Saunders, John, *widow and children*	Do.	25th Dec. 1813	4	48	
75	Sturdevant, Abisha, *widow*	Do.	4th Oct. -	4	48	Widow intermarried, June 15th, 1815.
76	Turner, Stephen, *widow*	1st lieutenant	25th July, 1814	15	180	
77	Tucker, William, *widow*	Private	5th May, 1813	4	48	
78	Tupper, Benj. *widow*	Do.	27th Nov. -	4	48	
79	Wheeler, Elijah, *widow*	Do.	13th Nov. -	4	48	
80	Woodman, Jos. *widow*	Do.	6th Nov. -	4	48	

B—Continued.

DISTRICT OF MAINE—*Continued.*

No.	Names of decedents, &c.	Rank or grade.	Original commencement of pension.	Pension per month.	Pension per annum.	Remarks, &c.
81	Wheeler, Samuel, *widow and children*	Private	3d Oct. 1813	$4 00	$48 00	Widow intermarried, November, 1816.
82	Wood, Thomas, *widow*	Do.	1st May, -	4	48	
83	Wetherell, John L. *widow*	Do.	1st Dec. -	4	48	
84	Wentworth, Jonathan, *widow*	Do.	1st Jan. 1814	4	48	
85	Westcot, Josiah, *widow*	Do.	24th Feb. 1813	4	48	
86	Willard, Caleb, *widow*	Do.	23d May -	4	48	
					$3,348 00	

B—Continued.

MASSACHUSETTS.

No.	Names of decedents, &c.	Rank or grade.	Original commencement of pension.	Pension per month.	Pension per annum.	Remarks, &c.
87	Andrews, Samuel, *widow*	Private	12th April, 1813	$4 00	$48 00	
88	Allard, Samuel, *widow*	Do.	26th Oct. -	4	48	
89	Burrows, Thomas, *widow and children*	Do.	26th Oct. -	4	48	Widow intermarried, Sept. 24th, 1814.
90	Bucklin, Joseph, *widow*	Captain	1st March, -	20	240	
91	Bradford, Lemuel, *widow*	Do.	17th Sept. 1814	20	240	
92	Coburn, Reubin, *widow*	Private	5th May, 1813	4	48	
93	Chapman, Jeremiah, *widow*	Captain	1st Jan. 1814	20	240	
94	Dewey, Samuel M. *widow*	Do.	29th Oct. 1813	20	240	
95	Dix, Timothy, *widow*	Lieut. colonel	14th Nov. -	30	360	
96	Farnham, Simon, *widow*	Private	29th May, -	4	48	
97	Howe, Daniel, *widow*	Do.	1st July -	4	48	
98	Haynes, Samuel, *widow*	Do.	20th Nov. -	4	48	
99	Kimball, Benj. *widow*	Musician	6th Aug. -	4 50	54	

B—Continued.

MASSACHUSETTS—Continued.

No.	Names of decedents, &c.	Rank or grade.	Original commencement of pension.	Pension per month.	Pension per annum.	Remarks, &c.
100	Leonard, John, *widow*	Private	20th Oct. 1815	$4 00	$48 00	
101	Lewis, William, *widow*	Do.	26th Oct. -	4	48	
102	Loring, Elisha, *widow and children*	Do.	26th Oct. -	4	48	Widow intermarried 27th Oct. 1816.
103	Lewis, Joseph, *widow*	Do.	3d Aug. -	4	48	Widow intermarried, 23d Aug. 1816.
104	M'Lucas, Jacob, *widow*	Do.	18th Oct. -	4	48	
105	Morey, Simeon, *children*	Sergeant	24th Jan. -	5 50	33	
106	M'Intire, Rufus, *widow*	Private	15th Feb. -	4	48	
107	Preble, Timothy, *widow*	Do.	28th Sept. -	4	48	
108	Phillips, Edward, *widow and children*	Do.	15th March -	4	48	

B—Continued.

MASSACHUSETTS—*Continued.*

No.	Names of decedents, &c.	Rank or grade.	Original commencement of pension.	Pension per month.	Pension per annum.	Remarks, &c.
109	Stephens, William, *widow*	Sadler	30th Dec. 1813	$6 50	$78 00	
110	Whitmore, Joseph, *widow*	Private	3d March,	4	48	
					$2,253 00	

B—Continued.

VERMONT.

No.	Names of decedents, &c.	Rank or grade.	Original commencement of pension.	Pension per month.	Pension per annum.	Remarks, &c.
111	Adye, William, *children*	Sergeant	20th Jan. 1814	$5 50	$66 00	
112	Beedle, Thomas, *widow*	Private	5th Dec. 1813	4	48	
113	Barnett, Job, do.	Do.	12th Jan. -	4	48	
114	Bixby, Ephraim, do.	Do.	6th Dec. -	4	48	
115	Baker, Benjamin T. do.	Corporal	11th Nov. -	5	60	
116	Bloomfield, Joseph, do.	Private	12th March, 1814	4	48	
117	Byram, David, do.	Do.	1st Nov. 1813	4	48	
118	Bowe, Stephen, do.	Do.	27th Aug. 1814	4	48	
119	Brewster, Ephraim, *widow and children*	Surgeon	11th Sept. 1812	22 50	270	Widow intermarried, 7th Dec. 1815.
120	Bingham, Jeremiah, *widow*	Private	9th March, 1813	4	48	
121	Bishop, Jesse, do.	Do.	4th Dec. 1812	4	48	See equalizing act of the 3d March, 1817.
122	Cross, Joseph, do.	Do.	30th July, 1813	4	48	
123	Corliss, John, do.	Do.	28th Nov. 1813	4	48	

B—Continued.

VERMONT—Continued.

No.	Names of decedents, &c.	Rank or grade.	Original commencement of pension.		Pension per month.	Pension per annum.	Remarks, &c.
124	Converse James, *widow*	Corporal	15th Sept.	1814	$5 00	$60 00	
125	French, Haines, do.	Major	1st Dec.	1813	25	300	
126	Goodrich, Valentine R. *widow and children.*	Captain	25th July,	1814	20	240	Widow intermarried, 15th March, 1815.
127	Green, Absolem, *widow*	1st lieutenant	18th Nov.	1812	15	180	
128	Haydon, Henry, do.	Private	1st Dec.	1813	4	48	
129	Hogins, James, do.	Do.	3d Dec.	1812	4	48	See equalizing act of March 3, 1817.
130	Hawley, Gideon, do.	1st lieutenant	3d June,	1816	15	180	Died of wounds.
131	Hunt, Daniel, do.	Private	9th March,	1814	4	48	
132	Hicks, Levi, do.	Do.	26th Jan.	1813	4	48	
133	Heath, David P. do.	Do.	5th March,	1814	4	48	
134	Hancock, Amasa, do.	Do.	18th Jan.	1814	4	48	
135	Jackson, David, do.	Do.	25th Jan.	1814	4	48	
136	Knight, Joseph, do.	Do.	18th Oct.	1813	4	48	

B—Continued.

VERMONT—Continued.

No.	Names of decedents, &c.	Rank or grade.	Original commencement of pension.	Pension per month.	Pension per annum.	Remarks, &c.
137	Lamphier, Thos. *widow*	Private	4th June, 1813	$4 00	$48	
138	Low, Obediah, do.	Do.	30th Aug. -	4	48	
139	Miles, Archaleous, do.	Do.	18th Jan. -	4	48	
140	Marshall, Silas, do.	Do.	8th Feb. 1814	4	48	
141	Miller, Samuel, do.	Do.	19th June, 1813	4	48	
142	Phelps, Mathew, do.	Major	5th Sept. -	25	300	
143	Robinson, Levi, do.	Private	12th March, -	4	48	
144	Sumner, Benjamin, do.	Do.	18th Aug. -	4	48	
145	Sanderson, Joel, do.	Do.	18th Nov. 1812	4	48	See equalizing act of March, 3, 1817.
146	Stanford, David do.	Do.	2d Sept. 1813	4	48	
147	Simmons, Benj. *widow* *and children*	Do.	10th Jan. 1814	4	48	Widow intermarried, Nov. 13, 1814.

B—Continued.

VERMONT—Continued.

No.	Names of decedents, &c.	Rank or grade.	Original commencement of pension.	Pension per month.	Pension per annum.	Remarks, &c.
148	Story, Joseph, *widow*	Private	29th Jan. 1814	$4 00	$48 00	
149	Sinkler, David, do.	Sergeant	20th May, 1813	5 50	66	
150	Tambling, Elisha, do.	Private	6th Dec. 1812	4	48	See equalizing act of 3d March, 1817.
151	Wescoat, Samuel, do.	Do.	27th Dec. 1813	4	48	
					$3,212 00	

B—Continued.

CONNECTICUT.

No.	Names of decedents, &c.	Rank or grade.	Original commencement of pension.	Pension per month.	Pension per annum.	Remarks, &c.
152	Bunnell, Samuel, *widow*	Private	12th Oct. 1813	$4 00	$48 00	
153	Forward, Daniel, do.	1st lieutenant	30th Oct. -	15	180	
154	Hall, Levi, do.	Private	15th Dec. -	4	48	
155	Hoadly, Luther, do.	Captain	8th Sept. -	20	240	
156	M'Lean, Charles, do.	1st lieutenant	28th April, -	15	180	
157	Nearing, Ashael, do.	Captain	20th Sept. -	20	240	
158	Olmstead, Ezekiel, do.	Private	30th Aug. -	4	48	
159	Reed, Chauncy, do.	Corporal	1st Jan. 1815	5	60	
					$1,044 00	

B—Continued.

RHODE ISLAND.

No.	Names of decedents, &c.	Rank or grade.	Original commencement of pension.	Pension per month.	Pension per annum.	Remarks, &c.
160	Greene, Ebenezer, *widow*	Private.	8th April, 1814	$4 00	$ 48 00	

NEW YORK.

No.	Names of decedents, &c.	Rank or grade.	Original commencement of pension.	Pension per month.	Pension per annum.	Remarks, &c.
161	Allen, Hanibal M. *widow*	Captain	11th May, 1813	20	240	
162	Adams, Daniel, *widow and children*	1st lieutenant	13th Oct. 1812	15	180	Widow intermarried, April 24, 1814.
163	Aldrick, Web, *widow*	Private	29th Nov. -	4	48	See equalizing act of 3d March, 1817.
164	Atkins, Ashael, do.	1st lieutenant	21st Dec. -	15	180	
165	Abbot, John, do.	Private	4th Feb. 1815	4	48	
166	Alexander, John, do.	Do.	8th Feb. 1813	4	48	
167	Benjamin, John, do.	Sergeant	18th Sept. 1814	5 50	66	

B—Continued.

NEW YORK—Continued.

No.	Names of decedents, &c.	Rank or grade.	Original commencement of pension.		Pension per month.		Pension per annum.		Remarks, &c.
168	Barnham, Elisha B. *widow*	Private	14th Oct.	1814	$4	0	$48	00	
169	Brown, Thomas, Jr. do.	1st lieutenant	17th Sept.	-	15		180		
170	Barrett, Peter, do.	Private	1st Dec.	-	4		48		
171	Bellinger, John, do.	Do.	1st Dec.	-	4		48		
172	Boyles, Philip, do.	Do.	28th Dec.	1812	4		48		See equalizing act of the 3d March, 1817.
173	Beebe, Ebenezer, *children*	Major	1st Sept.	1814	30		360		
174	Brown, David, *widow*	Private	29th Nov.	1812	4		48		See equalizing act of the 3d March, 1817.
175	Bartholomew, S. do.	Regt. surgeon	1st Dec.	1814	30		360		
176	Bassett, John, do.	Captain	3d Dec.	-	20		240		
177	Belknap, William, do.	2d lieutenant	17th Sept.	-	12	50	150		
178	Brown, James, *widow and children*	Private	10th Feb.	1813	4		48		Widow intermarried, 15th Feb. 1815.

B—Continued.

NEW YORK—Continued.

No.	Names of decedents, &c.	Rank or grade.	Original commencement of pension.		Pension per month.	Pension per annum.	Remarks, &c.
179	Bartlett, Henry, *widow*	Private	14th Oct.	1812	$4 00	$48 00	See equalizing act of the 3d March, 1817.
180	Bates, Benjamin, do.	Do.	14th Nov.	1814	4	48	Widow intermarried, 1st Dec. 1816.
181	Bacon, Joseph, do.	2d lieutenant	16th Nov.	-	12 50	150	See equalizing act of 3d March, 1817.
182	Berry, Elijah, do.	Private	4th Dec.	1812	4	48	
183	Barret, Samuel, do.	Do.	1st Feb.	1813	4	48	
184	Bachus, Electus, do.	Lieut. colonel	7th June,	-	30	360	
185	Boughton, Seymour, do.	Do.	30th Dec.	-	30	360	
186	Caldwell, Richard, do.	Captain	22d Nov.	1812	20	240	
187	Churchwell, Joseph, do.	Private	21st Oct.	1814	4	48	
188	Cheeseman, Wm. do.	Do.	30th Dec.	1813	4	48	
189	Clark, William, H. *widow and children.*	Do.	22d Nov.	1812	4	48	Widow intermarried, 8th Aug. 1813; see act 3d March, 1817.

B—Continued.

NEW YORK—Continued.

No.	Names of decedents, &c.	Rank or grade.	Original commencement of pensions.		Pension per month.		Pension per annum.		Remarks, &c.
190	Curtice, Daniel, *widow*	Captain	23d Nov.	1812	$20	00	$240	00	
191	Chappell, Joshua, do.	Sergeant	23d Sept.	1814	5	50	66		
192	Cadogan, Abraham, do.	Private	23d Nov.	-	4		48		
193	Curtis, Edmund, do.	Do.	17th Sept.	-	4		48		
194	Chadwick, Andrew do.	Do.	3d Dec.	1812	4		48		See act of March 3, 1817.
195	Cuyler, William H. do.	Maj. & aid de camp	9th Oct.	-	37		444		
196	Clark, Stephen, do.	Captain	13th Oct.	-	20		240		
197	Dunn, Ammon, do.	Sergeant	17th Sept.	1814	5	50	66		
198	Davis, James, do.	Private	7th Nov.	-	4		48		
199	Dupue, Samuel, do.	Do.	30th Dec.	1813	4		48		
200	Dudley, William C. *widow and children*	Major	30th Dec.	-	25		300		Widow intermarried April 13, 1815.
201	Dorance, George, *widow and children*	Private	18th Dec.	1812	4		48		Widow intermarried July 25, 1813, (see act 3d March, 1817.

30

B—*Continued.*

NEW YORK—Continued.

No.	Names of decedents, &c.	Rank or grade.	Original commencement of pension.	Pension per month.	Pension per annum.	Remarks, &c.
202	Dinsmore, Justin, *widow*	Private	22d Nov. 1812	$4 00	$ 48 00	See act 3d March, 1817.
203	Davis, Charles, do.	Musician	24th Oct. 1813	4 50	54	
204	Doty, William, do.	Private	11th Dec. 1812	4	48	See act of March 3d, 1817.
205	Davidson, John, do.	Captain	15th Feb. 1813	20	240	
206	Davis, Daniel, do.	Brig. general	17th Sept. 1814	52	624	
207	Emmons, Daniel, *widow and child*	Private	7th Dec. 1812	4	48	Widow intermarried Nov. 17, 1815, (see also act 3d March, 1817.)
208	Esgate, Jabez, *widow and children*	Sergeant	28th Sept. –	4	48	Do. do. Sept. 19, 1813.
209	Eaton, Ransom, *widow*	Do.	30th Nov. –	4	48	Do. do. Oct. 1, 1815.

B—Continued.

NEW YORK—Continued.

No.	Names of decedents, &c.	Rank or grade.	Original commencement of pension.	Pension per month.	Pension per annum.	Remarks, &c.
210	Fay, Hezekiah, *widow*	Private	18th June, 1815	$4	$ 48 00	Died in captivity.
211	Franklin, Sylvanus, do.	Do.	20th June, 1814	4	48	
212	Felton, Sylvanus, *children*	2d lieutenant	28th Aug. -	12 50	150	
213	Farren, John, *widow*	Private	28th July, 1813	4	48	
214	Ferall, Thomas, do.	Do.	5th Jan. -	4	48	
215	Faulkner, Arnold, do.	Do.	10th Nov. 1814	4	48	
216	Fenno, Moses, *widow and children*	Sergeant	30th Dec. 1813	5 50	66	Widow intermarried, 13th Oct. 1814.
217	Fairchild, Samuel, *widow*	Private	23d May, -	4	48	
218	Freeborn, Noel, do.	Do.	29th Oct. 1814	4	48	
219	Freer, Jacob, do.	Do.	10th Nov. -	4	48	
220	Gleason, Samuel, do.	Sergeant	23d March, 1813	5 50	66	
221	Hevnor, George, do.	Private	17th Sept. 1814	4	48	
222	Haisington, Job, do.	Do.	30th Dec. 1813	4	48	

B—Continued.

NEW YORK—Continued.

No.	Names of decedents, &c.	Rank or grade.	Original commencement of pension.	Pension per month.	Pension per annum.	Remarks, &c.
223	Hatstale, John, *widow*	Private	28th Oct. 1812	$4 00	$48 00	Widow intermarried, 9th June, 1816; (see also act 3d March, 1817.)
224	Hickcox, Vine W. *widow and children*	Sergeant	13th Oct. -	4	48	Do. do. 24th Dec.1815
225	Hawley, William, *widow and children*	Do.	30th Aug. -	4	43	Do. do. 14th July, 1814
226	Hathway, Daniel, *widow*	Captain	19th Jan. 1813	20	240	
227	Holmes, Isaac, do.	Private	22d Nov. 1814	4	48	
228	How, Edward, do.	Do.	17th Sept. -	4	48	
229	Humphrey, Chas. do.	Do.	28th Oct. -	4	48	
230	How, Darius, do.	Do.	16th Feb. 1813	4	48	
231	Horton, Elnathan, do.	Do.	1ᵗʰ Sept. 1814	4	48	
232	Heeny, Hugh, do.	Do.	10th May, 1813	4	48	
233	Hortan, Cyrus, do.	Do.	26th Jan. 1815	4	48	

B—Continued.

NEW YORK—*Continued.*

No.	Names of decedents, &c.	Rank or grade.	Original commencement of pension.		Pension per month.		Pension per annum.		Remarks, &c.
234	House, James, *widow*	Private	9th Nov.	1812	$4	00	$ 48	00	See act of March 3d, 1817.
235	Huntington, Reuben *widow and children*	Sergeant	21st Jan.	1813	5	50	66		Widow intermarried, 14th May, 1815.
236	Holt, Seth, *widow*	1st lieutenant	8th Nov.	1812	15		180		
237	Hatch, Charles O. do.	Private	18th April,	1813	4		48		
238	Ivory, William F. do.	Sergeant	8th Nov.	1812	4		48		
239	Jenkins, Hugh I. do.	Do.	27th Aug.	1814	5	50	66		
240	Johnson, John, do.	Private	25th Aug.	-	4		48		
241	Kenter Barnabas, do.	Corporal	7th Oct.	-	5		60		
242	King, Ezra, do.	Ensign	17th Nov.	1812	10		120		
243	Kinney, Charles, do.	Private	1st July,	1813	4		48		

B--Continued.

NEW YORK—Continued.

No.	Names of decedents, &c.	Rank or grade.	Original commencement of pension.	Pension per month.	Pension per annum.	Remarks, &c.
244	Keeler, Thomas, *widow and children*	Private	5th Dec. 1812	$4 00	$ 48 00	Widow intermarried, April 19th, 1816; see act 3d March, 1817.
245	Kenny, William, *widow*	Do.	23d July, 1813	4	48	
246	Lyon, Thomas, do.	Captain	27th April, -	20	240	
247	Lowe, Cornelius, do.	Private	14th Oct. 1812	4	48	See act of March 3d, 1817.
248	Laing, Drew, do.	Do.	18th Feb. 1815	4	48	
249	Linn, William, do.	Do.	7th Jan. -	4	48	
250	Lake, Andrew, do..	Do.	1st Jan. 1814	4	48	
251	Madden, Alpheus, do.	Do.	12th Sept. -	4	48	
252	Murray, Thomas, *widow and children*	Do.	15th June, 1813	4	48	Widow intermarried, 5th Feb. 1816.
253	Munger, Joseph, do.	Do.	17th Oct. 1814	4	48	

B—Continued.

NEW YORK—Continued.

No.	Names of decedents, &c.	Rank or grade.	Original commencement of pension.	Pension per month.	Pension per annum.	Remarks, &c.
254	McMichiel, Dan'l. *widow*	Private	25th Feb. 1813	$4 00	$48, 00	
255	Murphy, Joseph, do.	Do.	27th April, -	4	48	
256	McCullen, John, do.	Do.	10th Feb. 1815	4	48	
257	McDowle, John, *widow and children.*	Do.	2d Nov. 1812	4	48	Widow intermarried, 26th May, 1817; see act of March 3d, 1817.
258	McConnell, Malcomb, *widow,*	Do.	16th Sept. 1813	4	48	
259	Mills, John, *widow*	Lieut. colonel	29th May, 1813	30	360	
260	Nute, Obid, do.	Ensign	13th April, 1814	10	60	
261	Newkirk, Elias, do.	Private	28th Oct. -	4	48	
262	Nye, Stephen, do.	Do.	17th Sept. -	4	48	
263	Ousterhoudt, Peter T. do.	Sergeant	4th Nov. -	5 50	66	
264	O'Flyng, Temple E. *parents*	Ensign	17th Sept. -	10	120	See 3d sec. of an act of April 24, 1816.

B—Continued.

NEW YORK—Continued.

No.	Names of decedents, &c.	Rank or grade.	Original commencement of pension.	Pension per month.	Pension per annum.	Remarks, &c.
265	O'Flyng, Patrick, *parents*	2d Lieutenant	1st Nov. 1815	$12 50	$150 00	See 3d sect. of an act of April 24, 1816.
266	Post, Abraham, *widow*	Private	19th Oct. 1813	4	48	
267	Parson, Chester, do.	Sergeant	27th Sept. -	5 50	66	
268	Pierce, Barnabas, do.	Private	22d Oct. -	4	48	
269	Partridge, Stephen, do.	Do.	6th Sept. 1814	4	48	
270	Prentice, Menassah, do.	Ensign	20th Nov. -	10	20	
271	Passmore, Martin, do.	Private	10th Nov. -	4	48	
272	Pugh, Peter, do.	Corporal	1st Feb. 1813	5	60	
273	Row, Joseph L. do.	Private	17th Aug. 1814	4	48	
274	Russell, Henry, do.	Do.	30th Dec. 1813	4	48	
275	Robb, James, do.	Do.	24th March 1815	4	48	
276	Rosvelt, Thomas W. *widow and children*	1st Lieutenant	4th Sept. 1814	15	180	
277	Rush, John, *widow*	Private	29th Sept. -	4	48	
278	Risley, Chauncy, do.	Do.	17th Nov. -	4	48	

B—Continued.

NEW YORK—Continued.

No.	Names of decedents, &c.	Rank or grade.	Original commencement of pension.	Pension per month.	Pension per annum.	Remarks, &c.
279	Stone, Isaac W. *widow*	Lieut. Colonel	10th Sept. 1814	$30 00	360 00	
280	Seymour, Jacob, *widow and children*	Private	4th Sept. -	4	48	Widow died 31st January, 1845.
281	Smith, Enos, *widow*	1st Lieutenant	30th Sept. -	15	180	
282	Sadler, Henry, do.	Private	30th Dec. 1813	4	48	
283	Somers, Orum L. do.	Do.	2d Feb. 1815	4	48	
284	Smalley, or Smawley, Isaac, *widow*	Do.	14th Sept. 1814	4	48	
285	Small, Edward, do.	Do.	4th March 1815	4	48	
286	Stewart, John, do.	Do.	9th Nov. 1814	4	48	
287	Scofield, Samuel, do.	Hosp. surg. mate	8th June 1813	20	240	
288	Satterly, Phineas, *widow and children*	Private	15th Sept. 1814	4	48	Widow intermarried, 24th Feb. 1816.

B—Continued.

NEW YORK—Continued.

No.	Names of decedents, &c.	Rank or grade.	Original commencement of pension.	Pension per month.	Pension per annum.	Remarks, &c.
289	Seely, William, *widow and children*	Private	30th Dec. 1813	$4 00	$48 00	Widow intermarried, Aug. 22, 1814.
290	Selleck, James, *widow*	Captain	6th Jan. 1815	20	240	
291	Safford, Stephen, do.	Private	17th Sept. 1814	4	48	
292	Sage, Allen, *widow and children*	Farrier	20th Nov. 1812	4	48	Widow intermarried, March 1, 1817.
293	Staples, Joshua, *widow and children*	Private	25th Sept. 1814	4	48	
294	Spring, Darius, *widow*	Musician	17th Sept. 1814	4 50	54	Do. do. Aug. 6, 1815.
295	Smith, William, do.	Sergeant	19th Feb. 1813	5 50	66	
296	Stanton, Jonathan, do.	Private	11th Nov. 1814	4	48	
297	Sprague, Seth, do.	Do.	5th Dec. 1812	4	48	Widow intermarried, 8th Nov. 1816. (See act March 3, 1817.)

B—Continued.

NEW YORK—Continued.

No.	Names of decedents, &c.	Rank or grade.	Original commencement of pension.	Pension per month.	Pension per annum.	Remarks, &c.
298	Stoner, John, *widow*	Private	9th Nov. 1814	$4 00	$48 00	See act of March 3, 1817.
2c9	Smith, Coe, do.	Do.	31st Dec. 1812	4	48	
300	Swift, John, do.	Brig. general	13th July, 1814	52	624	
301	Saunders, Elisha S. do.	Captain	13th Oct. 1812	20	240	
302	Terry, Oliver; *widow and children*	Private	27th Nov.	4	48	Widow intermarried, April 27, 1814. (See act March 3, 1817.)
303	Tully, John H. *widow*	Sergeant	15th Feb. 1813	5 50	66	
5u4	Tupper, Ezra, do.	Private	22 June, 1813	4	48	
5u5	Watson, Simon Z. *widow and children*	Major	1st Sept. 1814	25	300	Widow intermarried, Feb. 25, 1816.
5u6	Wilcox, Israel, *widow*	3d lieutenant	1st May, 1813	11 50	138	
5u7	Westfall, Jacob, do.	Captain	13th Oct. 1812	20	240	

B—Continued.

NEW YORK—Continued.

No.	Names of decedents, &c.	Rank or grade.	Original commencement of pension.	Pension per month.	Pension per anuum.	Remarks, &c.
308	Woodruff, Chauncey, widow	Private	6th Sept. 1814	$4 00	$48 00	
309	Wright, Benjamin, do.	Do.	27th Dec. 1812	4	48	See act of March 3, 1817.
310	Wyckoff, Levi, do.	Do.	5th Oct. 1814	4	48	
311	Wallace, Abel, do.	Do.	25th Jan. 1815	4	48	
312	Wickham, Merrihew, do.	Do.	14th Nov. 1814	4	48	
313	Woodworth, Nathan, do.	Do.	30th Nov. -	4	48	
314	Worden, Walter, do.	Captain	11th Sept. -	20	240	
315	Whitney, Ezra, do.	Sergeant	20th Aug. 1812	4	48	
316	Woodman, Jeremiah, widow and children	Private	20th Feb. 1815	4	48	Widow intermarried, March 3, 1816.
317	Widner, Leonard, widow and children	Do.	27th Aug. 1814	4	48	Do. do. Aug. 30, 1815.
318	Wells, Russell, widow	Do.	8th Nov. 1813	4	48	

B—Continued.

NEW YORK—Continued.

No.	Names of decedents, &c.	Rank or grade.	Original commencement of pension.	Pension per month.	Pension per annum.	Remarks, &c.
319	Wilson, Eli, *widow*	3d lieutenant	12th Nov. 1814	$11 50	$138 00	
320	Waters, Peter, *widow and children*	Sergeant	17th Sept. -	5 50	66	Widow intermarried, Feb. 6, 1816.
321	Wood, Roswell, *widow and children*	Private	25th Oct. -	4	48	Do. do. Oct. 20, 1816.
322	White, Ebenezer, *widow*	Do.	10th May 1813	4	48	
323	Ward, Stephen, do.	Do.	15th Oct. 1814	4	48	
324	West, Joseph, do.	Asst. Apoy. gen.	17th Dec. -	22 50	270	
325	Webber, Henry, *widow and children*	Private	30th May, 1813	4	48	Widow intermarried, 10th Feb. 1815.
326	Williams, Dan. jr. *widow*	Do.	10th Nov. 1812	4	48	See act of March 3, 1817.
					$16,480 00	

B—Continued.

PENNSYLVANIA.

No.	Names of decedents, &c.	Rank or grade.	Original commencement of pension	Pension per month.	Pension per annum.	Remarks, &c.
327	Atkinson, Alexander, *widow*	Private	22d Sept. 1813	$4 00	$48 00	
328	Ackles, Jacob, do.	Do.	1st May, -	4	48	
329	Boyd, William, do.	Do.	19th March,1814	4	48	
330	Bell, Thomas, do.	Do.	6th July, 1813	4	48	
331	Baker, Anthony, *widow and children*	Do.	6th Feb. -	4	48	Widow died M y 30, 1815.
332	Carney, William, *widow*	Do.	5th Nov. -	4	48	
333	Conrad, Jacob, do.	1st lieutenant	10th April, -	15	180	
334	Delong, Henry, do.	Musician	17th March, -	4 50	54	
335	Ferree, Joel, do.	Lieut colonel	26th April, -	30	360	
336	Fisher, William, do.	Private	10th March, -	4	48	Widow intermarried, Dec. 25, 1814.
337	Fell, Mahlon, *widow and children*	Ensign	22d Jan.	10	120	Do. do. Jan. 21, 1816

B—Continued.

PENNSYLVANIA—Continued.

No.	Names of decedents, &c.	Rank or grade.	Original commencement of pension.	Pension per month.	Pension per annum.	Remarks, &c.
338	Gibson, James, *widow*	Colonel	17th Sept. 1814	$37 50	$450 00	
339	Hoffman, Isaac, do.	Corporal	18th May, 1813	5	60	
340	Hertzog, Frederick, do.	Sergeant	11th July, 1813	5 50	66	
341	Harvey, Folwell, do.	Private	3d Aug. 1812	4	48	See act of March 3, 1817.
342	Hatrick, William, do.	Do.	27th Nov. 1814	4	48	
343	Kummver, Abraham, do.	Do.	29th Oct. -	4	48	
344	Leopard, Jacob, do.	Do.	19th Aug. -	4	48	
345	Lynch, William, do.	Do.	9th July, 1813	4	48	
346	M'Clelland, Robert, do.	Do.	5th July, 1814	4	48	
347	M'Gee, John, do.	Do.	1st Nov. 1812	4	48	See act of March 3, 1817.
348	Olmstead, Edward, do.	1st lieutenant	11th Nov. 1813	15	180	
349	Province, Benjamin, do.	Private	11th Jan. 1814	4	48	
350	River, John, do.	Do.	5th Oct. 1813	4	48	
351	Robinson, Caleb, P. do.	2d lieutenant	28th Jan. 1815	12 50	1 50	

B—Continued.

PENNSYLVANIA—Continued.

No.	Names of decedents, &c.		Rank or grade.	Original commencement of pension.	Pension per month.	Pension per annum.	Remarks, &c.
352	Rice, John L.	*widow*	Private	7th Jan. 1814	$4 00	$48 00	
353	Shrader, John,	do.	Do.	25th Nov. -	4	48	
354	Taylor, John,	do.	Do.	1st Oct.	4	48	
355	Trindle, David,	do.	Do.	12th August -	4	48	
356	Tharp, Ichabod,	do.	Do.	1st May, 1813	4	48	
357	Vangorder, Elias,	do.	Do.	17th Feb. 1814	4	48	
358	Wolfkill, Henry,	do.	Do.	10th July, -	4	48	
359	White, John,	do.	Do.	7th April, 1813	4	48	
360	Warnick, John,	do.	1st lieutenant	11th Feb. 1814	15	180	
361	Wadsworth, Joseph, do.		Captain	15th April, 1813	20	240	
362	Walker, Robert,	do.	1st lieutenant	9th March, -	15	180	
						$3,372	

B—Continued.

NEW JERSEY.

No.	Names of decedents, &c.	Rank or grade.	Original commencement of pension.	Pension per month.	Pension per annum.	Remarks, &c.
363	Camman, Henry, *widow*	Private	28th Feb. 1814	$4 00	$48	
364	Cozier, Simon, do.	Do.	16th June, 1813	4	48	
365	Cramner, John, *widow and children*	Do.	1st March, -	4	48	Widow intermarried, Oct. 16, 1813.
366	Davis, Mahlon, *widow*	Major	17th Nov. 1814	25	$90	
367	Dunham, Benjamin, do.	Private	1st Dec. -	4	48	
368	Homan, or Howman, William, *widow and children*,	Do.	13th July, 1813	4	48	Widow intermarried, 14th Feb. 1816.
369	Ledew, Stephen, *widow and children*	Do.	13th June, -	4	48	Widow died October 2d, 1813.
570	Nestor, John, jun. *widow*	Do.	28th Nov. 1814	4	48	

32

B—Continued.

NEW JERSEY—Continued.

No.	Names of decedents, &c.	Rank or grade.	Original commencement of pension.		Pension per month.	Pension per annum.	Remarks, &c.
371	Ogdin, Israel, *children*	Corporal	6th Oct.	1814	$5 00	$60 00	
372	Sprogell, Thomas Y. *widow*						
373	Shepherd, Job, *widow*	Captain	1st Dec.	1813	20	240	
374	Turner, John, do.	Private.	30th Oct.	1814	4	48	
375	Thomas, Thomas, do.	Do.	19th Oct.	-	4	48	
		Do.	7th Dec.	1813	4	48	
						$1,080	

B—Continued.

DELAWARE.

No.	Names of decedents, &c.	Rank or grade.	Original commencement of pension.	Pension per month.	Pension per annum.	Remarks, &c.
376	Humphries, Rob't *widow*	Private	13th March, 1813	4	48	
377	Hurley, John, do.	Do.	2d March, 1814	4	48	
378	Nash, Nathaniel S. do.	Sergeant	15th March, 1814	5 50	66	
379	Stevens, Charles, do.	Private	29th May,	4	48	
					$ 210 00	

B—Continued.

MARYLAND.

No.	Names of decedents, &c.	Rank or grade.	Original commencement of pension.	Pension per month.	Pension per annum.	Remarks, &c.
380	Atwell, James, *widow*	Private	30th March, 1814	$4 00	$48 00	
381	Addison, William H. do.	Captain.	18th Dec. -	20	240	
382	Andre Gregorius, *widow and children*	1st lieutenant	12th Sept. -	15	180	Widow intermarried 8th Feb. 1817.
383	Bond, Benjamin, *widow*	Private	12th Sept. -	4	48	
384	Bowers, Jacob, do.	Do.	22th Nov. 1812	2 50	30	
385	Crea, Hugh, do.	Do.	13th Sept. 1814	4	48	
386	Davis, David, do.	Do.	16th Oct. -	4	48	
387	Dillon, James, do.	Captain	2d Oct. -	20	240	
388	Desk, Michael, do.	Private	12th Sept. -	4	48	
389	Donaldson,James L.do.	Lieut. and adj't.	12th Sept. -	20	240	
390	Evans, John, do.	Private	12th Sept. -	4	48	

B—Continued.

MARYLAND—Continued.

No.	Names of decedents, &c.	Rank or grade.	Original commencement of pension.	Pension per month.	Pension per annum.	Remarks, &c.
391	Earnest, Charles, *widow and children*	Private	31st Aug. 1816	$4 00	$ 48 00	Died of wounds. Widow intermarried, 20th January, 1817.
392	English, Marshall, *widow*	2d lieutenant	21st April, 1813	12 50	150	
393	Garrett, Thomas, do.	Private	13th Sept. 1814	4	48	
394	Creen, John, do.	Do.	23d Oct. 1814	4	48	
395	Grant, John, do.	Do.	28th April, 1813	4	48	
396	Hull, Edward, do.	Do.	24th Aug. 1814	4	48	
397	Haney, Thomas, do.	Do.	16th Aug. 1813	4	48	
398	Kithcart, Robert, do.	Do.	24th Sept. 1814	4	48	
399	Latham, Edward, do.	Do.	1st May, 1813	4	48	
400	Lee, James, do.	Do.	9th Nov. 1813	4	48	
401	Marriott, Elisha, do.	Sergeant	24th Aug. 1814	5 50	66	
402	Morgan, Loderwick, *child*	Major	12th Aug.	25	300	

B—Continued.

MARYLAND—Continued.

No.	Names of decedents, &c.	Rank or grade.	Original commencement of pension.		Pension per month.	Pension per annum.	Remarks, &c.
403	Mathews, Edward *widow*	Private	6th Sept.	1814	$ 4	$ 48 00	
404	M'Lean, Roger or Rhody, *widow*	Do.	8th April,	1813	4	48	
405	Mills, George, *widow*	Do.	26th June,	1813	4	48	
406	Martin, Anthony, do.	Do.	21st Oct.	1814	4	48	
407	M'Kenny, Philip, *widow and children*	Do.	1st Oct.	-	4	48	
408	Prosser Uriah, *widow*	Do.	12th Sept.	-	4	48	Widow intermarried, Dec. 14, 1815.
409	Prince, John, do.	Do.	21 Dec.	1813	4	48	
410	Routzong, John, do.	Do.	31st Jan.	1815	4	48	
						$ 2,550 00	

B—Continued.

VIRGINIA.

No.	Names of decedents, &c.	Rank or grade.	Original commencement of pension.	Pension per month.		Pension per annum.	Remarks, &c.
411	Alderton, John, *widow*	Private	26th Dec. 1814	$4		$48 00	
412	Ayres, Samuel, do.	Do.	5th Nov. -	4		48	
413	Allen, Andrew, do.	Do.	10th Oct. 1813	4		48	Widow intermarried,
414	Allen, William, do.	Do.	2d Dec. 1814	4		48	March 3, 1816.
415	Anderson, John, do.	Do.	15th Jan. 1813	4		48	
416	Arnold, George, *children*	Do.	28th Dec. 1812	4		48	See act of March 3,
							1817.
417	Anderson, Francis, *widow*	Do.	28th Feb. 1815	4		48	
418	Aydlet, or Idlet, David, *widow*	Drummer	24th May, 1813	4	50	54	
419	Ashby, George, do.	Corporal	1st August, 1814	5		60	
420	Allmond, Daniel, do.	Private	26th Nov. -	4		48	
421	Anderson, George, do.	Sergeant	12th Nov. -	5	50	66	
422	Anderson, Lewis,	Private	7th Nov. -	4		48	
423	Allen, William,	Do.	10th Sept. -	4		48	

B—Continued.

VIRGINIA—Continued.

No.	Names of decedents, &c.	Rank or grade.	Original commencement of pensions.		Pension per month.	Pension per annum.	Remarks, &c.
424	Bradey, Israel,	Private	4th Dec.	1814	$4 00	$48 00	
425	Bruner, Jacob,	Do.	22d Dec.	-	4	48	
426	Barlow, Jacob,	Do.	3d Dec.	1813	4	48	
427	Bussell, Randall,	Do.	12th Dec.	1814	4	48	
428	Burgess, Daniel,	Do.	13th Nov.	-	4	48	
429	Beagle, Joseph,	Do.	25th Dec.	-	4	48	
430	Boatright, John, *widow*	Do.	20th Dec.	1814	4	48	
431	Bartlett, Thomas, do.	Sergeant	21st Oct.	-	5 50	66	
432	Beheler, John, do.	Private	1st March,	-	4	48	
433	Butler, James, do.	Do.	15th Dec.	-	4	48	
434	Boyd, Robert, do.	Do.	30th Sept.	-	4	48	
435	Bolling, or Bouldin, Thomas, do.	Do.	1st April,	1815	4	48	
436	Bishop, Joseph C. do.	Do.	1st Jan.	1814	4	48	
437	Bird, Thomas, do.	Do.	1st Oct.	-	4	48	
438	Brooks, William, do.	Do.	30th July,	-	4	48	

B—Continued.

VIRGINIA—Continued.

No.	Names of decedents, &c.	Rank or grade	Original commencement of pension.	Pension per month.	Pension per annum.	Remarks, &c.
439	Beard, Robert, *widow*	Private	1st Nov. 1814	$4 00	$48 00	
440	Brill, Henry, do.	Do.	12th Dec. -	4	48	
441	Beard, Samuel, do.	Do.	2d Jan. 1815	4	48	
442	Bishop, Mathew, do.	Do.	16th July, 1814	4	48	
443	Brumfield, Joshua, do.	Do.	51st Dec. -	4	48	
444	Blades, John, do.	Do.	15th Dec. -	4	48	
445	Butcher, James, do.	Do.	16th Sept. -	4	48	
446	Baynham, William, do.	Do.	28th Nov. -	4	48	
447	Bugg, Anslem, do.	Do.	28th Oct. -	4	48	
448	Barrett, John, do.	Do.	24th Jan. 1815	4	48	
449	Bowden, Robert, do.	Sergeant	2d Sept. 1814	5 50	66	
450	Booker, John, *children*	Private	31st Aug. -	4	48	
451	Barnes, John, *widow*	Do.	5th Dec. -	4	48	
452	Bains, James, do.	Do.	28th Dec. -	4	48	
453	Bowers, David, *widow and children*	Do.	15th Oct. -	4	48	} Widow died, Oct. 20, 1814.

33

B—Continued.

VIRGINIA—Continued.

No.	Names of decedents, &c.	Rank or grade.	Original commencement of pension.	Pension per month.	Pension per annum.	Remarks, &c.
454	Bean, Walter, *widow*	Private	1st Feb. 1814	$4 00	$48 00	
455	Bowen, Charnel, do.	Do.	8th Nov. -	4	48	
456	Brittain, Beale, do.	Do.	20th Sept. -	4	48	
457	Bendall, James, do.	Do.	17th Oct. -	4	48	
458	Bagby, William, do.	Do.	18th Dec. -	4	48	
459	Bailiss, John, do.	Do.	18th Aug. -	4	48	
460	Burke, Edmond, do.	Corporal	28th July, 1813	5	60	
461	Brooks, Warren J. do.	Private	3d Jan. 1814	4	48	
462	Burress, Andrew, do.	Do.	25th Oct. -	4	48	
463	Brockwell, William, do.	Do.	26th Sept. -	4	48	
464	Britt, Obediah, do.	Do.	30th April, -	4	48	
465	Billiter, Caleb, do.	Do.	21st Dec. -	4	48	
466	Bushong, Jacob, do.	Do.	24th Oct. -	4	48	
467	Corbin, Adam, do.	Do.	20th Nov. -	4	48	
468	Candiff, John G. do.	Do.	27th Dec. -	4	48	

B—Continued.

VIRGINIA—Continued.

No.	Names of decedents, &c.	Rank or grade.	Original commencement of pension.	Pension per month.	Pension per annum.	Remarks, &c.
469	Clybourn, or Cliburn, Leonard, *widow*	Private	15th Sept. 1814	$4 00	$48 00	
470	Cooper, Leonard, do.	-	29th Jan. 1815	4	48	
471	Cottrell, Andrew, do.	-	1st Feb. 1813	4	48	
472	Carner, William, do.	-	3d Dec. 1814	4	48	
473	Casey, Thomas, do.	-	18th Jan. 1815	4	48	
474	Church, William, do.	-	26th Oct. 1814	4	48	
475	Carsley, Richard, do.	Corporal	15th July, -	5	60	
476	Clever, Stephen, do.	Private	27th Dec. -	4	48	
477	Cardwell, Humph. W. do.	-	7th Sept. -	4	48	
478	Claiborne, Leonard, do.	-	30th Oct. -	4	48	
479	Cook, George, do.	-	10th Sept. -	4	48	
480	Calahan, James, do.	-	16th July, 1813	4	48	
481	Crews, Thomas, do.	-	25th Nov. 1814	4	48	
482	Cheatham, Hezekiah, do.	-	6th Oct. 1813	4	48	
483	Curry, George, do.	-	13th Jan. 1815	4	48	

B—Continued.

VIRGINIA—Continued

No.	Names of decedents, &c.	Rank or grade.	Original commencement of pension.	Pension per month.	Pension per annum.	Remarks, &c.
424	Cooper, John, *widow*	Private	2d July, 1813	$4 00	$48 00	
485	Conner, Michael, do.	-	17th Aug. 1814	4	48	
486	Crawford, Martin, do.	-	26th Oct. -	4	48	
487	Cox, Erskine, *widow and child*	-	1st Dec. -	4	48	Widow intermarried. Dec. 14, 1815.
488	Cason, Bartlett, *widow*	-	19th Oct. 1813	4	43	
489	Claiborne, Robert, do.	-	22d Dec. 1814	4	48	
490	Cole, John, do.	-	17th March, -	4	48	
491	Debusk, Daniel, do.	-	22d Dec. -	4	43	
492	Daniel, John M. do.	Hospital surgeon	8th Oct. 1813	37 50	450	
493	Dawson, John, do.	Private	6th Dec. 1814	4	48	Widow intermarried April 18, 1816.
494	Donahowan, or Dunahoo, Geo. *widow*	-	28th Dec. -	4	48	
495	Donahoe, Henry, do.	-	21st Nov. -	4	48	

B—Continued.

VIRGINIA—Continued.

No.	Names of decedents, &c.	Rank or grade.	Original commencement of pension.	Pension per month.	Pension per annum.	Remarks, &c.
496	Dickinson, John, *widow*	Private	10th Sept. 1814	$4 00	$48 00	
497	Dunn, Walters, do.	-	19th Dec. -	4	48	
498	Dangerfield, John, do.	-	6th Nov. -	4	48	
499	Darby, John, do.	-	28th Aug. -	4	48	
500	Dann, John W. do.	-	30th April, 1813	4	48	
501	Dame, William B. do.	-	13th Sept. 1814	4	48	
502	Doughtry, Thomas, do.	-	3d Aug. 1813	4	48	
503	Deem, Abraham, do.	-	14th Jan. 1815	4	48	
504	Dicksenson, Reed, do.	-	15th Oct. 1814	4	48	
505	Drake, Silas, do.	-	27th Oct. -	4	48	
506	Davis, Jabez, do.	-	20th Oct. -	4	48	
507	Dobyn, Griffin, do.	-	20th Jan. 1815	4	43	
508	Durham, Nicholas, do.	-	19th April, 1814	4	48	
509	Davenport, Glover, do.	-	28th Nov. -	4	48	
510	Dickson, Pleasant, *widow and children*	-	5th Sept. -	4	48	} Widow intermarried, Sept. 20, 1816.

B.--Continued.

VIRGINIA—Continued.

No.	Names of decedents, &c.		Rank or grade.	Original commencement of pension.	Pension per month.	Pension per annum.	Remarks, &c.
511	Dailey, Enoch,	widow	Private	3d Oct. 1814	$4 00	$ 48 00	Widow intermarried, 29th March, 1815.
512	Daniel, John,	do.	Do.	30th Jan. -	4	48	
513	Davis, Mathew,	do.	Do.	17th Oct. -	4	48	
514	Dye, Vincent,	do.	Do.	20th Dec. -	4	48	
515	Drennen, John	do.	Do.	5th Dec. -	4	48	
516	Dixon, John,	do.	Do.	9th Oct. -	4	48	
517	Daniel, Thomas,	do.	Do.	17th Dec. -	4	48	
518	Dyer, John,	do.	Do.	12th Dec. -	4	48	
519	Ellinger, George,	do.	Do.	18th Sept. -	4	48	
520	Early, Joshua,	do.	Captain	3d Nov. -	20	240	
521	Eubank, Garland	do.	Private	1st Nov. -	4	48	
522	Eudaly, William,	do.	Do.	3d Sept. 1813	4	48	
523	Eubank, Warner,	do.	Do.	1st April, -	4	48	
524	Fry, Jacob,	do.	Captain	15th Sept. 1814	20	240	
525	Foreacres, James,	do.	Private	24th Nov. -	4	48	

B—Continued

VIRGINIA—Continued.

No.	Names of decedents, &c.	Rank or grade.	Original commencement of pension.	Pension per month.	Pension per annum.	Remarks, &c.
526	Fletcher, John, *widow*	Private	9th Jan. 1815	$4 00	$48 00	
527	Fields, James, do.	Do.	14th April, 1814	4	48	
528	Flood, Charles, do.	Corporal	26th Oct. -	5	60	
529	Flesher, Peter, do.	Private	26th Nov. -	4	48	
530	Fawley, Anthony, do.	Do.	1st Feb. 1815	4	48	
531	Farmer, Burwell, do.	Do.	6th April, 1814	4	48	
532	Farley, Henry, do.	Do.	30th Nov. -	4	48	
533	Goren, Hanson, do.	Do.	1st Dec. -	4	48	
534	Goslin, Ezekiel, do.	Do.	1st Jan. 1815	4	48	
535	Goul, Adam, do.	Do.	21st Jan. 1815	4	48	
536	Gresham, Benjamin, do.	1st Lieutenant	3d Sept. 1814	15	180	
537	Garvin, David, *children*	Corporal	25th Dec. 1814	5	60	
538	Gilliland, Samuel, *widow*	Sergeant	18th Jan. 1815	5 50	66	
539	Green, John, do.	Private	12th Dec. 1814	4	48	
540	Grove, Jacob, do.	Do.	8th Jan. 1815	4	48	

B—Continued.

VIRGINIA—Continued.

No.	Names of decedents, &c.	Rank or grade.	Original commencement of pension.	Pension per month.	Pension per annum.	Remarks, &c.
541	Goodrich, Shadrick, or Meshiduc, widow	Corporal	25th July, 1814	$ 5 00	$60 00	
542	Green, William, do.	Private	8th Dec. 1813	4	48	
543	Goode, John, do.	-	27th Aug. 1814	4	48	
544	Galloway, William, do.	-	18th Feb. 1814	4	48	
545	Goldsborough Thomas, do.	-	31st Jan. -	4	48	
546	Groves, Daniel, do.	Musician	14th Dec. -	4 50	54	
547	Galt, John M. do.	Captain	6th Feb. 1815	20	240	
548	Gaines, James, do	Private	8th May, 1813	4	48	
549	Garrett, Richard G. do	-	31st Aug. 1814	4	48	
550	Godley, Edmund, do.	-	8th Jan. 1815	4	48	
551	Hurst, Benjamin, do.	-	19th Nov. 1814	4	48	
552	Harding, Elijah, do.	Captain	17th Dec. -	20	240	
553	Hodge, John, do.	Private	17th Nov. -	4	48	
554	Hutchinson, Andrew, do.	-	12th Jan. 1815	4	48	

B—Continued.

VIRGINIA—Continued.

No.	Names of decedents, &c.	Rank or grade.	Original commencement of pension.	Pension per month.	Pension per annum.	Remarks, &c.
555	Holder, John, *widow*	Private	11th Dec. 1814	$ 4 00	$ 48 00	
556	Hemphill, Samuel, do.	-	14th Nov. -	4	48	
557	Huston, Joseph, do.	Sergeant	25th Dec.	5 50	66	
558	Helvy, Jacob, do.	Private	3d Nov. -	4	48	
559	Humphrees, Henry, do.	-	20th Dec. -	4	48	
560	Hardy, George, do.	-	6th August, -	4	48	
561	Hilman, William, do.	-	14th Sept. -	4	48	
562	Harwell, Mark, do.	-	3d Nov. -	4	48	
563	Harris, Charles, do.	Sergeant	27th Jan. 1815	5 50	66	
564	Hall, John, do.	Private	30th Sept. 1813	4	48	
565	Humphreys, John, *widow and children*	2d lieutenant	3d August, 1814	12	150	Widow intermarried, March 28, 1816.
566	Hundley, Caleb, *widow*	Private	14th Oct. -	4	48	
567	Harris, William, do.	-	12th Nov. -	4	48	

34

B—Continued.

VIRGINIA—Continued.

No.	Names of decedents, &c.	Rank or grade.	Original commencement of pension.		Pension per month.	Pension per annum.	Remarks, &c.
568	Harison, Wylie, *widow*	Private	21st Jan.	1815	$4 00	$48 00	
569	Hargrove, Josiah, do.	-	10th Oct.	1814	4	48	
570	Howell, Jacob, do.	-	1st May,	-	4	48	
571	Hulvey, Philip, do.	Corporal	13th Feb.	1815	5	60	Widow intermarried, April 4th, 1816.
572	Hughs, Emory, do.	Private	1st Jan.	-	4	48	
573	Hight, Joseph, do.	-	10th Dec.	1814	4	48	Do. do. April 10, 1816.
574	Heflin, Martin, do.	-	28th Dec.	-	4	48	
575	Hodges, Nathaniel, *widow and children*	-					
576	Houchens, Bennett, *widow*	-	1st July,	1813	4	48	Do. do. April 2, 1814.
577	Hunter, Robert, do.	-	1st Nov.	1814	4	48	
578	Henry, William, do.	-	23d Nov.	1813	4	48	Do. do. Dec. 19, 1816.
579	Hillard, John, do.	-	21st Nov.	1814	4	48	Do. do. 1st Aug. 1816.
580	Jackson, Hugh, do.	-	8th Aug.	1813	4	48	
			1st Oct.	1814	4	48	

B—Continued.

VIRGINIA—Continued.

No.	Names of decedents, &c.	Rank or grade.	Original commencement of pension.	Pension per month.	Pension per annum.	Remarks, &c.
581	Johnson, John, *widow*	Private	11th Sept. 1814	$4 00	$48	
582	Johnson, David, do.	-	13th Dec. -	4	48	
583	Jaco, William, do.	-	10th Nov. -	4	48	
584	Johnson, William, do.	-	20th Oct. 1813	4	43	
585	Johnson, Julius, do.	2d lieutenant	15th Oct -	12 50	150	
586	Johnson, Samuel, *widow and child*	Private	8th Nov. 1814	4	48	
587	Joiner, Baker, *widow*	-	20th June, 1813	4	48	
588	Johnson, Mathew, do.	-	18th July, 1814	4	48	
589	Jeffries, Pleasant, do.	-	6th Nov. -	4	48	
590	Jenkins, Henry, do.	-	5th June 1813	4	48	
591	Jennison, Alexander, do.	-	8th Dec. 1814	4	48	
592	Jan es, Robert, *widow and children*	Cornet	10th Sept. 1813	10	120	
593	Jeffries, George *widow*	Corporal	18th Nov. 1814	5	60	

B—Continued.

VIRGINIA—Continued.

No.	Names of decedents, &c.	Rank or grade.	Original commencement of pension.		Pension per month.		Pension per annum.	Remarks, &c.
594	Karnes, John, *widow*	Private	28th Dec.	1814	$4 00		$48 00	
595	King, Joseph, do.	-	8th Jan.	1815	4		48	
596	Kezee, or Kizzee, or Kize, George, *widow*	-						
597	Kizer, Abednigo, do.	-	15th Dec.	1814	4		48	
			4th Oct.	-	4		48	
598	Kelly, Michael, do.	-	9th Oct.	-	4		48	
599	Koontz, Jacob, do.	2d lieutenant	6th May,	1815	12 50		150	
600	Kittle, George, do.	Private	17th Nov.	1814	4		48	
601	Kitchen, Job, do.	-	9th Nov.	-	4		48	
602	Kephart, Henry, do.	-	20th Nov.	-	4		48	
603	Kingery, Peter, do.	-	14th Nov.	-	4		48	
604	Kackley, Elias, do.	Sergeant	3d Dec.	-	5 50		66	
605	King, William, sen. do.	Private	2d Feb.	-	4		48	
606	Kite, Daniel, do.	-	11th Sept.	-	4		48	
607	Knox, William, do.	-	13th Oct.	-	4		48	

B—Continued.

VIRGINIA—Continued.

No.	Names of decedents, &c.	Rank or grade.	Original commencement of pension.	Pension per month.	Pension per annum.	Remarks, &c.
608	Kemp, William, *widow*	1st lieutenant	15th Dec. 1814	$15 00	$180 00	
609	Kersey, John, jun. do.	Private	2d Nov. -	4	48	
610	Lyndsay, John, do.	-	7th Oct. -	4	48	
611	Laiton, William, do.	-	19th Dec. -	4	48	
612	Lynch, George, do.	-	2d Dec. -	4	48	
613	Lewis, Joshua, do.	-	22d March, -	4	48	
614	Laffoon, Nathaniel, do.	-	13th Dec. -	4	48	
615	Lewis, Edward, do.	-	24th Dec. -	4	48	
616	Law, Burwell, jr. *widow and child*		5th Dec. 1813	4	48	
617	Leforce, Monsier, *widow*	-	5th Oct. 1814	4	48	
618	Leftwich, Uriah, do.	2d lieutenant	16th Sept. 1812	12 50	150	
619	Lewis, Coleman, do.	Private	1st Dec. 1814	4	48	
620	Longest, Carter, do.	-	25th June, 1813	4	48	
621	Laugherly, William, do.	-	6th Dec. 1814	4	48	
622	Lane, Joel, do.	Ensign	16th Sept. -	10	120	

B—Continued.

VIRGINIA—Continued.

No.	Names of decedents, &c.	Rank or grade.	Original commencement of pension.		Pension per month.		Pension per annum.		Remarks, &c.
623	Land, John, *widow*	Private	6th April,	1814	$4	00	$48	00	
624	Ligon, Richard W. do.	-	14th Dec.	-	4		48		
625	Morgan, Zackquil, do.	Captain	24th Aug.	-	20		240		
626	M‘Cartney, John, do.	1st lieutenant	12th Oct.	-	15		180		
627	Morriss, John, do.	Private	6th Jan.	1815	4		48		
628	Morrison, William, do.	Sergeant	7th Oct.	1814	5	50	65		
629	Markwood, Jacob, do.	Drum major	13th Jan.	1815	5	50	66		
630	Murdock, John, do.	Sergeant	7th Sept.	1814	5	50	66		
631	Morgan, Charles, do.	Private	25th Dec.	-	4		48		
632	M‘Gehu, John, do.	-	10th Nov.	-	4		48		
633	Mullins, Jesse, do.	-	12th April,	-	4		48		
634	May, John, do.	-	24th Dec.	-	4		48		
635	May, Frederick, do.	-	1st Jan.	1815	4		48		
636	M‘Laughlin, William, do.	-	5th Dec.	1814	4		48		
637	Mann, John, do.	-	16th Nov.	-	4		48		
638	M‘Erae, Anthony, do.	-	1st Aug.	-	4		48		

B—Continued.

VIRGINIA— Continued.

No.	Names of decedents, &c.	Rank or grade.	Original commencement of pension.		Pension per month.	Pension per annum.	Remarks, &c.
639	Maddera, John F. *widow*	Private	16th Feb.	1814	$4 00	$ 48 00	
640	Moore, Henry, do.	-	3d Feb.	1815	4	48	
641	Murphy, Thomas, do.	-	7th Dec.	1814	4	48	
642	Mayo, Robert, do.	-	10th March,	-	4	48	
643	M'Clung, Samuel, do.	-	26th July,	-	4	48	
644	Moore, Littlebury, do.	-	25th Aug.	-	4	48	
645	Mays, Thomas, do.	-	16th Sept.	-	4	48	
646	M'Culloch, or M'Cully, John, *widow*	-	21st Oct.	1813	4	48	
647	Mitchell, William, do.	-	30th Sept.	1814	4	48	
648	M'Haney, Richard H. *widow and children*	-	2d Dec.	-	4	48	Widow intermarried, Jan. 24, 1816.
649	Mauzey, Thomas, *widow*	-	19th Dec.	-	4	48	
650	Mayfield, Jesse, do.	-	25th Sept.	-	4	48	
651	Mosley, John, do.	-	14th Jan.	1815	4	48	

B—Continued.

VIRGINIA—Continued.

No.	Names of decedents, &c.	Rank or grade.	Original commencement of pension.		Pension per month.	Pension per annum.	Remarks, &c.
652	M'Laurine, Joseph, *widow*	Captain	9th Sept.	1814	20	$ 24 00	
653	Merryman, John T. do.	Private	12th Sept.	-	4	48	
654	Martin, Cary, do.	-	1st March,	1815	4	48	
655	Messeck, John, do.	-	15th Feb.	1814	4	48	
656	Murray, John, do.	-	7th April,	1813	4	48	
657	Moore, Alexander, do.	-	6th Aug.	1814	4	48	
658	Merideth, Joseph, do.	-	25th Nov.	1813	4	48	
659	M'Ewing, or M'Cuin,	-	18th Nov.	1814	4	48	
	Thomas, *widow*	-					
660	Mussleman, Joseph, do.	-	28th Nov.	-	4	48	
661	M'Kay, William, do.	-	3d Jan.	1815	4	48	
662	M'Daniel, Simeon, do.	-	19th Dec.	1814	4	48	Widow intermarried, Oct. 26, 1817.
663	Musgrove, Joseph, do.	-	24th Dec.	-	4	48	
664	Morgan, Evan S. *widow and child*	-	26th Aug.	-	4	48	Do. do. July 11, 1816.

B—Continued.

VIRGINIA—Continued.

No.	Names of decedents, &c.	Rank or grade.	Original commencement of pension.		Pension per month.	Pension per annum.	Remarks, &c.
665	M'Guffin, James, widow	Private	27th Aug.	1813	$4 00	$48 00	
666	Noel, Jacob, do.	-	22d May,	1814	4	48	
667	Nelson, Benum, do.	-	12th Nov.	-	4	48	
668	Nicolls, George, do.	-	5th Dec.	-	4	48	
669	North, Philip, do.	-	5th Dec.	-	4	48	
670	Night, or Knight, George, widow						
671	Overstreet, Jesse, do.	-	8th Dec.	-	4	48	
672	O Dear, William, do.	-	7th Oct.	-	4	48	
673	Powell, Henry, do.	-	1st Sept.	-	4	48	
674	Payne, William, do.	-	14th Dec.	-	4	48	
675	Payne, Lewis, do.	-	20th Oct.	-	4	48	
676	Powell, Charles G. do.	Ensign	5th Dec.	-	4	48	
677	Perkins, John, do.	Private	24th Nov.	-	10	120	
678	Payne, or Pain, George, widow		19th Dec.	-	4	48	
679	Powell, Benjamin, do.	-	19th Nov.	-	4	48	
			17th Dec.	-	4	48	

B—Continued.

VIRGINIA—Continued.

No.	Names of decedents, &c.	Rank or grade.	Original commencement of pension.		Pension per month.	Pension per annum.	Remarks, &c.
680	Persel, or Perselly, Richard, *widow*	Private	1st Oct.	1814	$4	$48 00	
681	Phillips, John, do.	-	26th Oct.	-	4	48	
682	Pumphrey, John, do.	-	1st Feb.	1815	4	48	
683	Price, Thomas M. do.	-	22d July,	1814	4	48	
684	Previte, Asa, do.	-	25th Dec.	-	4	48	
685	Parsons, William, do.	-	26th Dec.	1813	4	48	
686	Power, John, do.	-	25th June,	-	4	48	
687	Perine, James, do.	-	11th Dec.	1814	4	48	
688	Penninger, Jacob, do.	Corporal	24th Oct.	1813	5	60	
689	Phifer, James, do.	Private	22d Sept.	1814	4	48	
690	Pratt, James, do.	-	6th Nov.	-	4	48	
691	Payne, John, do.	-	18th Oct.	-	4	48	
692	Perkins, James, do.	-	11th August	-	4	48	
693	Patton, Nimrod, do.	Musician	17th Nov.	-	4 50	54	

B—Continued.

VIRGINIA—Continued.

No.	Names of decedents, &c.	Rank or grade.	Original commencement of pension.	Pension per month.	Pension per annum.	Remarks, &c.
694	Propst, Henry, *widow*	Private	17th Oct. 1813	$4 00	$48 00	Widow intermarried, 17th May, 1816.
695	Price, Thomas, do.	Sergeant	2d Nov. 1814	5 50	66	
696	Redshaw, William, do.	Private	7th Nov. -	4	48	
697	Ruckman, Samuel, do.	Corporal	4th June, 1813	5	60	
698	Raney, Ezekiel, do.	Private	11th March 1815	4	48	
699	Ridgeway, William do.	-	1st Nov. 1813	4	48	
700	Rodes, Jacob, do.	-	1st Oct. 1814	4	48	
701	Ryburn, James, do.	-	15th Sept. -	4	48	
702	Robey, James, do.	-	21st Sept. 1813	4	48	
703	Rigney, Isham, do.	-	14th Jan. 1815	4	48	
704	Riffle, George, do.	-	15th March, 1815	4	48	
705	Richardson, Thos. do.	-	27th Oct. 1814	4	48	
706	Roten, or Roughton, William, *widow*	-	12th Nov. -	4	48	

B—Continued.

VIRGINIA—Continued.

No.	Names of decedents, &c.	Rank or grade.	Original commencement of pension.		Pension per month.	Pension per annum.	Remarks, &c.
707	Roten, or Roughten, James, *widow*	Private	5th Dec.	1814	$4 00	$48 00	
708	Roller, John, *widow*	do.	9th Dec.	-	4	48	
709	Richardson, James, do.	do.	2d Sept.	-	4	48	
710	Starky, Edward, do.	do.	10th Sept.	-	4	48	
711	Scott, Thomas, do.	do.	29th Nov.	-	4	48	
712	Smith, Samuel, do.	do.	5th Nov.	-	4	48	
713	Semones, Stephen, do.	do.	24th Jan.	-	4	48	
714	Stickleman, John, do.	do.	31st Oct.	-	4	48	
715	Sheets, Frederick, do.	do.	20th Nov.	-	4	48	
716	Shipley, Benjamin do.	Ensign	27th March,	1813	10	120	
717	Snider, David, do.	Private	9th Dec.	-	4	48	
718	Steeman, John, do.	-	10th Nov.	1814	4	48	
719	Stratton, Thomas, do.	1st Lieutenant	15th Nov.	-	15	180	
720	Stuart, Jesse, do.	Private	19th Nov.	-	4	48	

B—Continued.

VIRGINIA—Continued.

No.	Names of decedents, &c.	Rank or grade.	Original commencement of pension.		Pension per month.		Pension per annum.		Remarks, &c.
721	Sharp, Robert, *widow*	Private	28th Oct.	1814	$4	00	$48	00	
722	Shelton, James, do.	Captain	20th Nov.	-	20		240		
723	Shelton, Frederick, do.	Private	20th Dec.	1813	4		48		
724	Sims, Austin, do.		27th Oct.	1814	4		48		
725	Shelton, Nathan, do.	Sergeant	12th Jan.	-	5	50	66		
726	Stephens, George, do.	Private	31st Dec.	-	4		48		
727	Spencer, William, do.	-	25th Nov.	-	4		48		
728	Shackelford, Leonard D. *widow*	-	26th Aug.	-	4		48		
729	Stone, John, do.	-	3d Oct.	-	4		48		
730	Supinger, John, do.	-	20th Nov.	-	4		48		
731	Stone, Asuer, do.	-	24th July,	1813	4		48		
732	Shackelford, Christ. do.	-	30th June,	1814	4		48		
733	Strader, John, do.	-	1st Dec.		4		48		
734	Suter, James, do.	-	31st Dec.	-	4		48		
735	Stump, Henry, **do.**	-	12th Nov.	-	4		48		

B—Continued.

VIRGINIA—Continued.

No.	Names of decedents, &c.	Rank or grade.	Original commencement of pension.	Pension per month.	Pension per annum.	Remarks, &c.
736	Scott, William, *widow*	Private	9th March, 1814	$4 00	$ 48 00	
737	Smith, John, jun. do.	-	17th Dec. -	4	48	
738	Thompson, Benona, do.	-	14th Nov. -	4	48	
739	Teany, John, do.	-	11th Jan. 1815	4	48	
740	Thoma, John, do.	-	1st Feb. -	4	48	
741	Teal, Henry, do.	-	1st Dec. 1814	4	48	
742	Taylor, Wm. sen. do.	-	6th Jan. -	4	48	
743	Taylor, James, do.	-	14th Jan. -	4	48	
744	Tenny, William, do.	-	1st Nov. -	4	48	
745	Taylor, Nicholas, do.	-	1st Nov. 1813	4	48	
746	Thompson, Pleasant, do.	-	28th May, 1814	4	48	
747	Tomlinson, James, do.	-	26th Dec. -	4	48	
748	Taylor, William, do.	-	14th July, -	4	48	
749	Taylor, John, do.	-	6th July, -	4	48	
750	Thom, Micajah A. do.	Sergeant	4th Dec. -	5 50	66	

B--Continued.

VIRGINIA—*Continued.*

No.	Names of decedents, &c.	Rank or grade.	Original commencement of pension.		Pension per month.	Pension per annum.	Remarks, &c.
751	Vance, Robert, *widow*	Private	24th Jan.	1814	$4 00	$ 48 00	
752	Vincent, Richard, do.	-	21st Dec.	-	4	48	
753	Widener, Frederick John, *widow*	-	5th Jan.	1815	4	48	
754	White, James, do.	-	18th Jan.	1814	4	48	
755	Wright, or Right, James, *widow*						
756	Westfall, Isaac, do.	-	3d Jan.	1815	4	48	
757	Watkins, Henry, do.	-	22d Nov.	1814	4	48	
758	Woods, Mathew, do.	-	29th Jan.	1815	4	48	
759	Willis, Bennet, do.	Corporal	16th Oct.	1814	4	48	
760	Wood, James, do.	Private	18th Jan.	-	5	60	
761	Wilson, Thomas, do.	-	17th Oct.	-	4	48	
762	Williams, James, do.	-	6th Dec.	-	4	48	
763	Wheeler, James, do.	-	16th March, -		4	48	
			10th Jan.	1815	4	48	

B—Continued.

VIRGINIA—Continued

No.	Names of decedents, &c.	Rank or grade.	Original commencement of pension.	Pension per month.	Pension per annum.	Remarks, &c.
764	Wilson, Jacob, *widow*	Private	5th Feb. 1815	$4 00	$48 00	
765	Wier, Thomas, do.	-	20th Sept. 1813	4	48	
766	Warren, John, do.	-	27th Aug. 1814	4	48	
767	Wilson, Samuel, do.	-	1st Sept. -	4	48	
768	Webley, John, do.	-	30th Aug. -	4	48	
769	Ward, Richard, do.	-	24th Dec. -	4	48	
770	Wilkes, William, jr. do.	Corporal	9th Dec. -	5	60	
771	Wilson, Joseph, do.	Private	8th Jan. 1815	4	48	
772	Wiseman, Benjamin, do.	-	4th Dec. 1814	4	48	
773	Williams, Hugh, do.	-	26th Aug. -	4	48	
774	Wright, William, do.	-	15th Dec. -	4	48	
775	Woodruff, Jesse, do.	-	19th Oct. -	4	48	
776	Weathers, Nathan, do.	Sergeant	26th Aug. -	5 50	66	
777	Whitlock, Robert, do.	Private	23d Nov. -	4	48	
778	White, Littlebury, do.	-	10th Nov. 1813	4	48	

B—Continued.

VIRGINIA—Continued.

No.	Names of decedents, &c.	Rank or grade.	Original commencement of pension.	Pension per month.	Pension per annum.	Remarks, &c.
779	Whitmore, James, *widow*	Private	15th Oct. 1814	$4 00	$48 00	
780	Young, James, do.	-	5th Dec. -	4	48	
781	Yates, James, do.	-	6th Dec. -	4	48	
782	Yates, Reuben C. do.	2d lieutenant	10th Sept. -	12 50	150	
783	Zircle, John, do.	Private	4th Dec. -	4	48	
					21,390	

36

B—Continued.

NORTH CAROLINA.

No.	Names of decedents, &c.	Rank or grade.	Original commencement of pension.	Pension per month.	Pension per annum.	Remarks, &c.
784	Aslin, David, *widow*	Private	13th Feb. 1815	$4 00	$48 00	
785	Alphin, Jesse, do.	-	15th Nov. 1814	4	48	
786	Burton, David, do.	-	31st Oct. -	4	48	
787	Brown, Edward, do.	-	12th Sept. -	4	48	
788	Barker, John, do.	-	28th Dec. -	4	48	
789	Ballard, William, do.	-	6th Jan. 1815	4	48	
790	Banes, William, do.	-	8th Jan. -	4	48	
791	Butler, Silas, do.	-	14th Jan. -	4	48	
792	Congleton, William, do.	-	23d Dec. 1814	4	48	
793	Carter, Isaac, do.	-	1st March, 1815	4	48	
794	Cannon, James, *child*	-	14th Feb. 1815	4	48	
	Carlisle, William, *widow*	-	3d Feb. -	4	48	
795	Hodge, Joshua, do.	-	21st Jan. -	4	48	
796	Hicks, Daniel, do.	-	1st Feb. -	4	48	
797						

B—Continued.

NORTH CAROLINA—Continued.

No.	Names of decedents, &c.		Rank or grade.	Original commencement of pension.	Pension per month.	Pension per annum.	Remarks, &c.
798	Hayes, James,	*widow*	Private	11th Feb. 1815.	$4 00	$48	
799	Ham, Benjamin,	do.	-	28th Jan. -	4	48	
800	Hamilton, Jesse,	do.	-	28th Nov. 1814	4	48	
801	Howell, Stephen,	do.	-	12th Jan. 1815	4	48	
802	Ivery, Charles,	do.	-	16th March, 1813	4	48	
803	Knighten, James,	do.	-	15th Feb. 1813	4	48	
804	Lyon, Zachariah,	do.	-	15th Jan. 1815	4	48	
805	M'Quiston, Robert,	do.	Captain	10th March, -	20	240	
806	M'Farland, James,	do.	Private	14th Jan. -	4	48	
807	Meezle, or Mizell, James,	*widow*	-				
808	Oaks, Samuel,	do.	-	24th Oct. 1814	4	48	
809	Overton, Jacob,	do.	-	13th Feb. 1815	4	48	
810	Phillip, Leonard,	do.	-	15th Jan. -	4	48	
811	Page, Silas,	do.	f	2d March, -	4	48	

B—Continued.

NORTH CAROLINA—Continued.

No.	Names of decedents, &c.	Rank or grade.	Original commencement of pension.	Pension per month.	Pension per annum.	Remarks, &c.
812	Parish, John, *widow*	Private	22d March, 1815	$4 00	$48 00	
813	Pridgin, Peter, do.	-	5th Jan. 1815	4	48	
814	Pope, Archibald, do.	-	27th Oct. 1814	4	48	
815	Roberts, Willis, do.	-	1st March, 1815	4	48	
816	Sullivan, Whittenton, do.	-	1st March, 1815	4	48	
817	Shearly, Kelly, do.	-	19th Feb. -	4	48	
818	Simmons, Malichi, do.	-	2d Feb. -	4	48	
819	Shelfer, John, do.	-	10th March	4	48	
820	Simmons, Samuel, do.	-	1st Jan. -	4	48	
821	Vaughan, Nichoias, do.	-	21st Dec. 1813	4	48	
822	Worsham, Henry, do.	-	1st March, 1815	4	48	
823	Williams, Richard, do.	-	9th Feb. -	4	48	
824	White, Thomas W. do.	Sergeant	14th Jan. -	5 50	66	

3,178

B—Continued.

SOUTH CAROLINA.

No.	Names of decedents, &c.	Rank or grade.	Original commencement of pension.	Pension per month.	Pension per annum.	Remarks, &c.
825	Cox, John F. widow	Private	2d Feb. 1815	$ 4 00	$48 00	
826	Hendricks, Nathan, do.	-	12th June, 1814	4	48	
827	Long, Isaac, do.	Corporal	26th March, 1815	5	60	
828	Murray, Daniel, do.	Private	29th Nov. 1813	4	48	
829	Moore, Robert B. do.	Major	17th Sept. 1814	25	300	
830	Madden, John T. widow and children	Private	12th Aug. 1812	4	48	Widow intermarried, Feb. 22, 1814; (see also act 3d March, 1817.)
831	Noble, James, widow	2d lieutenant	21st July, 1814	12 50	150	
832	Park, William, do.	Sergeant	5th March, 1815	5 50	66	
833	Rochester, Reuben, do.	Private	15th June, 1814	4	48	
834	Riseuer, Isaac, do	-	11th Feb. -	4	48	
835	Scoggins, George, do.	-	27th Feb. -	4	48	

B.—Continued.

SOUTH CAROLINA—Continued.

No.	Names of decedents, &c.	Rank or grade.	Original commencement of pension.	Pension per month.	Pension per annum.	Remarks, &c.
856	Sanders, John, do.	Private	15th Feb. 1815	$ 4 00	$ 48 00	
857	Willard, Prentice, *widow and child*	Captain	13th Oct. 1813	20	240	Widow intermarried Oct. 16, 1816.
					$ 1,200 00	

B—Continued.

GEORGIA.

No.	Names of decedents, &c.	Rank or grade.	Original commencement of pension.	Pension per month.	Pension per annum.	Remarks, &c.
835	Allen, George, *widow*	Private	21st Feb. 1815	$4 00	$48 00	
839	Butts, Samuel, do.	Captain	28th Jan. 1814	20	240	
840	Brown, Jacob, do.	Private	1st March, -	4	48	
841	Blackwell, do.	-	5th Jan. -	4	48	
842	Bowen, Hukey, do.	-	24th Dec.	4	48	
843	Crawford, John, do.	-	5th Feb. 1815	4	48	
844	Coffee, Reuben, do.	-	20th March, 1814	4	48	
845	Gilmore, William, do.	Ensign	9th May, 1815	10	120	
846	Hagins, James, do.	Private	10th Dec. 1813	4	48	
847	Harrison, Benj'n D. do.	-	23d Nov. 1814	4	48	
848	Jarrett, Nicholas, do.	-	7th March, 1815	4	48	
849	Jennings, Rial do.	-	23d Feb. -	4	48	
850	Owen, William, do.	Captain	15th Feb. 1814	20	240	
851	Parker, Mathew G. do.	Private	22th Nov. 1813	4	48	

B—Continued.

GEORGIA—*Continued.*

No.	Names of decedents, &c.	Rank or grade.	Original commencement of pension.	Pension per month.	Pension per annum.	Remarks, &c.
852	Phillip, Bartholomew, *widow*	Private	10th Nov. 1814	$4 00	$ 48 00	
853	Self, Willis, do.	-	4th Dec. 1813	4	48	
					$1,224 00	

B—Continued.

KENTUCKY.

No.	Names of decedents, &c.	Rank or grade.	Original commencement of pension.	Pension per month.	Pension per annum.	Remarks, &c.
854	Allison, Alexander, *widow*	Private	5th May, 1815	$ 4 00	$ 48 00	
855	Alexander, Wm. P. do.	1st lieutenant	3d Feb. 1815	15	180	
856	Archibald, Wm. do.	Private	1st July, 1813	4	48	
857	Allen, John,	Lieut. Colonel.	22d Jan. -	30	360	
858	Brim, James, do	Private	20th Nov. -	4	48	
859	Banks, Reuben, *widow and children*	-	2d June, -	4	48	Widow intermarried, 23d Feb. 1814.
860	Ball, William, *widow*	-	5th May, -	4	48	
861	Bradburne, Joseph, do.	-	5th May, -	4	48	
862	Bruce, James, do.	-	16th Oct. -	4	48	
863	Baxter, Samuel, do.	-	3d Nov. 1812	4	48	
864	Beata, Abraham, do.	-	5th Oct. 1813	4	48	See act of March 3d, 1817.
865	Bartlett, Foster, do.	-	4th Oct. 1813	4	48	

37

B—Continued.

KENTUCKY—Continued.

No.	Names of decedents, &c.	Rank or grade.	Original commencement of pension.	Pension per month.	Pension per annum.	Remarks, &c.
866	Brian, James, *widow*	Private	22d Jan. 1813	$ 4 00	$ 48 00	
867	Baker, Henry, do.	-	15th Nov. -	4	48	
868	Bear, John, do.	-	22d Dec. 1814	4	48	
869	Burgess, Henry, do.	-	5th Sept. 1813	4	48	
870	Beard, Philip, do.	-	4th March, 1814	4	48	
871	Brissey, John, *widow and children*	-	15th Dec. 1812	4	48	See act of March 3d, 1817. (Widow intermarried Aug. 1, 1813.)
872	Bowman, Wm. *widow*	-	1st May, 1815	4	48	
873	Blackburn, John, do.	-	22d Jan. 1813	4	48	
874	Burris, Joseph, do.	Sergeant	24th March, 1815	5 50	66	
875	Pailey, John, do	Private	21st March, 813	4	48	
876	Blake, Thomas, do.	-	10th March, 1814	4	48	
877	Bledsoe, Jacob, do.	-	1st May, -	4	48	

B—Continued.

KENTUCKY—Continued.

No.	Names of decedents, &c.	Rank or grade.	Original commencement of pension.	Pension per month.	Pension per annum.	Remarks, &c.
878	Bridges, William, *widow*	Private	1st Nov. 1813	$4 00	$48 00	
879	Barnes, John, do.	-	21st Dec. -	4	48	
880	Bartlett, John C. do.	Qr. M. General	1st Jan. 1814	37 50	450	
881	Bealer, Henry, *widow and child*	Private	1st June, 1813	4	48	Widow intermarried, 15th Oct. 1813.
882	Clutter, Paul, *widow*	-	4th Nov. -	4	48	
883	Craig, Elijah, do.	-	14th Oct. -	4	48	
884	Clinkeibeard, Joseph, do.	-	4th May, -	4	48	
885	Corbin, James, do.	-	5th May, -	4	48	
886	Campbell, Lindsay, *children*	Sergeant	11th May, -	5 50	66	
887	Coleman, Thomas, *widow and children*	1st Lieutenant	1st Dec. 1812	15	180	Widow intermarried, 18th June, 1816.
888	Crouch, Isaac, *widow*	Private	8th Jan. 1815	4	48	

B—Continued.

KENTUCKY—Continued.

No.	Names of decedents, &c.	Rank or grade.	Original commencement of pension.	Pension per month.	Pension per annum.	Remarks, &c.
889	Collins, Lewis, *widow*	Private	17th Sept. 1813	$4 00	$48 00	
890	Callahan, John, do.	-	5th May, -	4	48	
891	Crook, James, do.	-	5th May, -	4	48	
892	Cooper, John, do.	Sergeant	5th May, -	5 50	66	
893	Crosby, Overton, do.	Private	5th March, 1815	4	48	
894	Cotrill, Thomas, do.	-	10th Dec. 1813	4	48	
895	Clines, Nicholas, do.	-	22d Jan. -	4	48	
896	Chapman, Benjamin, do.	-	1st Dec. -	4	48	
897	Constable, Thomas, do.	-	5th May, -	4	48	
898	Coy, Daniel, do.	-	10th April, 1815	4	48	
899	Cash, William, *widow and children*	-	2d March, -	4	48	
900	Calvert, Thomas, *children*	-	22d Dec. 1813	4	48	
901	Coplinger, Solomon, *widow*	-	22d Jan. -	4	48	

B—Continued.

KENTUCKY—Continued.

No.	Names of decedents, &c.	Rank or grade.	Original commencement of pension.		Pension per month.	Pension per annum.	Remarks, &c.
902	Cole, David, *widow*	Private	1st June	1813	$4 00	$48 00	
903	Cook, William, do.	-	31st July,	-	4	48	
904	Carlisle, Henry, do.	-	1st Dec.	1812	4	48	See act of March 5, 1817.
905	Clark, Joseph, do.	Captain	5th May,	1813	20	240	
906	Campbell, John B. do.	Colonel	28th Aug.	1814	37 50	450	
907	Daniel, William G. do.	Private	5th May,	1813	4	48	
908	Dobyns, John, do.	1st lieutenant	1st Dec.	-	15	180	
909	Dyhouse, Edward, do.	Private	29th Sept.	-	4	48	
910	Dickerson, William, *widow and children*	1st lieutenant	1st Nov.	-	15	180	Widow intermarried, July 27, 1815.
911	Dixon, Henry, *widow*	Private	30th Nov.	-	4	48	
912	Degarnett, John, *widow and children*	-	27th Nov.	1812	4	48	Widow intermarried, Nov. 26, 1818.

B—Continued.

KENTUCKY—Continued.

No.	Names of decedents, &c.	Rank or grade.	Original commencement of pension.		Pension per month.		Pension per annum.		Remarks, &c.
913	Demoss, John, *widow*	Private	25th June, 1813		$4	00	$48	00	
914	Drum, Phillip, *widow and children*	-	3d May	-	4		48		Widow intermarried, April 30, 1817.
915	Dotson, Thomas, *widow*	-	15th Jan.	1815	4		48		
916	Duncan, Fielding, do.	-	30th May,	1813	4		48		
917	Dooly, Ephraim, do.	1st lieutenant	5th May,	-	15		180		
918	Davis, Thomas C. do.	Surgeon	22d Jan.	-	22	50	270		
919	Dudley, William, do.	Colonel	5th May,	-	37	50	450		
920	Daviess, Joseph H. do.	Major	7th Nov.	1811	30		360		
921	Easter, William, do.	Private	5th May,	1813	4		48		
922	Embrey, Elijah, do.	-	22d April,	1815	4		48		
923	Ellis, William, *children*	Captain	1st Jan.	1813	20		240		
924	Evans, Willian, *widow*	Private	15th May,	1814	4		48		
925	Eubank, James T. do.	Asst. D. P. M.	7th Dec.	1814	20		240		

B—Continued.

KENTUCKY—Continued.

No.	Names of decedents, &c.	Rank or grade.	Original commencement of pension.	Pension per month.	Pension per annum.	Remarks, &c.
926	Elkins, Ellitt, *widow*	Private	5th May, 1813	$4	$48 00	
927	Eslick, Joseph, do.	-	30th Jan. 1814	4	48	
928	Etherington, James, do.	-	22d Jan. 1813	4	48	
929	Elliott, Elijah, do.	-	2d July, -	4	48	
930	Elliott, James, do.	-	5th May, -	4	48	
931	Edwards, Robert, do.	Captain	22d Jan. -	20	240	
932	Edwards, Elisha, *widow and children*	1st lieutenant	22d Nov. 1812	15	180	Widow intermarried, July 30, 1815.
933	Forrest, Memorial, do.	Captain	15th March, 1815	20	240	
934	Francis, Thomas, do.	Private	5th July, 1815	4	48	
935	Field, Risen, or Reuₗen, *widow*	-	26th Dec. 1814	4	48	
936	French, Joseph, do.	-	21st Feb. 1815	4	48	
937	Fletcher, Thomas, do.	-	27th Sept. 1815	4	48	

B—Continued.

KENTUCKY—Continued

No.	Names of decedents, &c.	Rank or grade.	Original commencement of pension.	Pension per month.	Pension per annum.	Remarks, &c.
938	Flynn, Peter, *widow*	Private	22d Jan. 1813	$4 00	$ 48 00	
939	Gon, William, do.	-	19th Jan. -	4	48	
940	Goodman, William B. do.	-	3d Nov. -	4	48	
941	Glore, Reuben, do.	-	5th May, -	4	48	
942	Grace, Henry, do.	-	8th Feb. 1815	4	48	
943	Gwinn, David, do.	Corporal	22d Jan. 1813	5	60	
944	Graham, William, do.	Private	25th Jan. 1815	4	48	
945	Groves, Edward, do.	-	9th May, 1813	4	48	
946	Galligher, James, do.	-	22d Oct. -	4	48	
947	George, Joseph, do.	Sergeant	5th May, -	5 50	66	
948	Gray, Patrick, do.	Captain	27th Feb. -	20	240	
949	Graves, Benjamin, do.	Major	22d Jan. -	25	300	
950	Hawkins, Archelous, do.	Private	26th July, -	4	48	
951	Hull, Jeham, do.	-	5th May -	4	48	
952	Hill, William, do.	-	9th Oct. -	4	48	

B—Continued.

KENTUCKY—Continued.

No.	Names of decedents, &c.	Rank or grade.	Original commencement of pension.		Pension per month.		Pension per annum.		Remarks, &c.
953	Hawkins, Basilla, *widow*	Private	17th Jan.	1814	$4	00	$48	00	Widow intermarried, Dec. 10, 1814.
954	Harris, Sherwood, do.	-	5th May,	1813	4		48		
955	Hughs, David, do.	-	5th May,		4		48		
956	Hyser, Philip, do.	-	14th July,	1814	4		48		
957	Hutcherson, Samuel, do.	-	22d Jan.	1813	4		48		
958	Hall, William, do.	-	5th May,	-	4		48		
959	Harris, Thomas, do.	-	5th May,	-	4		48		
960	Howard, Mathew, do.	-	22d Jan.	-	4		48		
961	Huston, James, do.	Sergeant	9th Dec.	-	5	50	66		
962	Hammond, John, do.	Private	14th Dec.	1814	4		48		
963	Hollowday, Bazel, do.	-	22d Jan.	1813	4		48		
964	Havens, Benjamin, do.	-	31st Dec.	1814	4		48		
965	House, Moses, do.	-	5th May,	1813	4		48		
966	Henderson, Joseph, do.	-	15th Nov.	-	4		48		

38

B—Continued.

KENTUCKY—Continued.

No.	Names of decedents, &c.	Rank or grade.	Original commencement of pension.	Pension per month.	Pension per annum.	Remarks, &c.
967	Harrold, William, *widow*	1st Lieutenant	23d Feb. 1815	$15 00	$180 00	
968	Hopkins, Mordica, do.	Private	22d Jan. 1813	4	48	
969	Harris, William, do.	Ensign	30th Oct. -	10	120	
970	Hutchenson, Charles, do.	Private	5th May -	4	48	
971	Hutchison, Charles, do.	-	18th Oct. 1812	4	48	See act of March 3, 1817.
972	Hadden, Hugh, do.	-	24th March, 1815	4	48	
973	Hickman, Paschal, do.	Captain	22d Jan. 1813	20	240	
974	Hart, Nathaniel G. S. *widow*	Capt. and Dept. Inspt. Gen.	22d Jan. -	20	240	See act of March, 1817.
975	Jones, Richard, do.	Private	1st Jan. 1814	4	48	
976	Johnson, Thomas, *widow and children*	-	16th May, 1813	4	48	Widow intermarried, July 20, 1818.
977	Jascoby, Frederick, *widow*	-	22d Jan. 1813	4	48	

B—Continued.

KENTUCKY—Continued.

No.	Names of decedents, &c	Rank or grade.	Original commencement of pension.	Pension per month.	Pension per annum.	Remarks, &c.
978	Johnson, Major, *widow*	Private	5th Dec. 1813	$4 00	$48 00	
979	Jones, Elijah, or Elisha, *widow*					
980	Judd, James, *widow*	-	5th May, 1813	4	48	
981	Irwin, John, do.	-	11th June, -	4	48	
982	Kile, or Kyle, John, do.	Hos. surgeon	22d Jan. -	37 50	450	
983	Kendrick, Lewis, do.	Private	5th Feb. 1814	4	48	
984	Killbreath, John, do.	-	15th Oct. 1813	4	48	
985	Kenny, James, do.	Captain	5th May, 1813	20	240	
986	Kertly, Beverly, do.	Private	31st Jan. -	4	48	
987	Kincheloe, Lewis, *widow and children*	-	7th Dec. -	4	48	
	Knapp, Charles, *widow*	Major	1st Dec. -	25	30	Widow intermarried 24th Dec. 1815.
	Kinder, George, do.	Private	4th March, 1815	4	48	
		-	22d Jan. 1813	4	48	

B—Continued.

KENTUCKY—Continued.

No.	Names of decedents, &c.	Rank or grade.	Original commencement of pension.	Pension per month.	Pension per annum.	Remarks, &c.
990	Logan, Samuel, *widow*	2d lieutenant	10th Oct. 1813	$12 50	$ 150 00	
991	Lightfoot, Philip, *chil-dren,*		5th May, -	5	60	
992	Linchard, Thomas, *widow*	Corporal	30th Dec. -	4	48	
993	Lawson, Thomas, do.	Private	22d Jan. -	4	48	
994	Lee, James, do.	-	9th Dec. -	4	48	
995	Langham, William, do.	-	16th Nov. 1814	4	48	
996	Lewis, Hugh, do.	-	14th Feb. 1815	4	48	
997	Lewis, Thomas, do.	Captain	5th May, -	20	240	
998	M'Bride, Lapsley, do.	Private	22d Jan. 1813	4	48	
999	Manifee, Gaydon, do.	Corporal	5th May, -	5	60	
1000	Malone, John, do.	Private	5th May, -	4	48	
1001	M'Ginnis, Hezekiah, do.	-	18th May, -	4	48	
1002	Mefford, Andrew, do.	-	22d Jan. -	4	48	
1003	Miller, William, do.	-	1st Nov. 1812	4	48	

B—Continued.

KENTUCKY—Continued.

No.	Names of decedents, &c.	Rank or grade.	Original commencement of pension.	Pension per month.	Pension per annum.	Remarks, &c.
1004	M'Clelland, Wm. *widow*	Corporal	14th Dec. 1813	$5 00	$ 60 00	
1005	M'Connell, Wm. do.	Private	5th March, -	4	48	
1006	Moon, Nathan, do.	-	15th May, -	4	48	
1007	M'Mahon, John, do.	Captain	26th Dec. 1814	20	240	
1008	Maxwell, William, do.	-	5th May, 1813	4	48	
1009	M'Michael, John, do.	-	30th Oct. 1812	4	48	See act of March 3d, 1817.
1010	Morton, Archibald, do.	-	26th Nov. 1813	4	48	
1011	Martin, Peter, do.	-	6th Oct. 1814	4	48	
1012	Mahurin, John, do.	-	22d Jan. 1813	4	48	
1013	Mulligan, Berryman do.	-	22d Jan. -	4	48	
1014	Mitchell, Samuel, do.	-	22d Jan. -	4	48	
1015	M'Kinney, Thomas do.	-	23d June, -	4	48	
1016	Miiler, John, do.	-	22d Jan. -	4	48	
101?	Miller, John, do.	-	18th April, 1814	4	48	

B—Continued.

KENTUCKY—Continued.

No.	Names of decedents, &c.	Rank or grade.	Original commencement of pension.		Pension per month.		Pension per annum.		Remarks, &c.
1018	Morgan, Peter, *widow*	Private	31st May,	1813	$4	00	$48	00	
1019	M'Kee, Robert, do.	-	21st July,	-	4		48		
1020	Morriss, John, do.	-	25th March,	1814	4		48		
1021	M'Cue, Edward, do.	-	5th May,	1813	4		48		
1022	Milton, Jacob, do.	-	27th Feb.	1814	4		48		
1023	Marrs, Samuel, do.	-	31st Jan.	1815	4		48		
1024	M'Cracken, Virgil, *widow and child*	Captain	22d Jan.	1813	20		240		Widow intermarried, 24th Jan. 1816.
1025	Maxwell, Joseph, *widow*	Private	7th Nov.	1811	3	33	39	96	See act of April 10th, 1812.
1026	Norman, Calebo, do.	-	5th May,	1813	4		48		
1027	Norris, John, do.	Sergeant	5th May,	-	5	50	66		
1028	..ealy, John, do.	Private	14th Nov.	1812	4		48		See act of March 3d, 1817.
1029	Nall, William. H, do.	-	22d Jan.	1813	4		48		

B—Continued.

KENTUCKY—*Continued.*

No.	Names of decedents, &c.	Rank or grade.	Original commencement of pension.	Pension per month.	Pension per annum.	Remarks, &c.
1030	Nortrep, John, *widow*	Corporal	18th Oct. 1812	$ 3 50	$42 00	Widow intermarried 22d May, 1817.
1031	Overton, Moses, do.	Private	5th April, 1815	4	48	
1032	Odle, Reuben, do.	-	21st Nov. 1813	4	48	
1033	Overluse, Jacob, *widow and child*	-	1st Nov. -	4	48	Widow intermarried, June 1st, 1815.
1034	Philley, Roger, *widow*	Sergeant	23d Jan. 1815	5 50	66	
1035	Pitts, Joseph, do.	Private	22d Jan. 1813	4	48	
1036	Price, Samuel, do.	Captain	4th Nov. -	20	240	
1037	Pulliam, Benjamin, do.	Private	10th Dec. -	4	48	
1038	Frice, Richard, do.	2d lieut and adj't.	11th Nov. -	12 50	150	See act of March 3d, 1817.
1039	Plough, William, do.	Private	5th May, -	4	48	
1040	Peck, James, do.	-	23d May, -	4	48	

B—Continued.

KENTUCKY—Continued.

No.	Names of decedents, &c.	Rank or grade.	Original commencement of pension.		Pension per month.	Pension per annum.	Remarks, &c.
1041	Porter, Benjamin, *widow*	Sergeant	22d Jan.	1813	$5 50	$66	
1042	Padgitt, James, do.	Private	22d Jan.	-	4	48	
1043	Pullam, John, do.	-	29th Dec.	1814	4	48	
1044	Paxton, Robert, do.	Captain	28th Feb.	1815	20	240	
1045	Plummer, George do.	Private	22d Jan.	1813	4	48	Widow intermarried, 31st May, 1815.
1046	Price, James C. do.	Captain	22d Jan.	-	20	240	
1047	Pike, Zebulon M. do.	Brig. general	27th April,	-	52	624	
1048	Quarles, Samuel, do.	Private	22d Jan.	-	4	48	
1049	Right, Edward, do.	-	5th May,	-	4	48	
1050	Robinson, George, do.	-	22d Jan.	-	4	48	
1051	Richardson, Jesse, do.	-	15th Oct.	-	4	48	
1052	Rollins, Ezekiel, do.	-	5th May,	-	4	48	
1053	Rogers, James, do.	-	6th Nov.	-	4	48	
1054	Raney, Abraham, do.	-	22d Jan.	-	4	48	

B—Continued.

KENTUCKY—Continued.

No.	Names of decedents, &c.	Rank or grade.	Original commencement of pension.		Pension per month.	Pension per annum.	Remarks, &c.
1055	Roberts, Pleasant M. widow	Private	22d Jan.	1813	$ 4 60	48	
1056	Rice, George, do.	-	1st June,	-	4	48	
1057	Rodgers, John, do.	-	2 th Oct.	-	4	48	
1058	Robbins, David, do.	-	14th Dec.	1814	4	48	
1059	Ryon, John, do.	-	22d Jan.	1813	4	48	
1060	Rankin, Benjamin, do.	-	22d Jan.	-	4	48	
1061	Rayburn, John, do.	-	9th March,	1815	4	48	
1062	Rawford, Robert, do.	Corporal	22d Jan.	1813	5	60	
1063	Scott, John M	Lieut. colonel	26th Dec.	1812	30	360	
1064	Stroude, Samuel,	Private	10th May,	1815	4	48	See act of March 3d, 1817.
1065	Sadler, James, do.	-	28th August	-	4	48	
1066	Simmons, David, do.	-	20th Dec.	1812	4	48	
1067	Sloan, Daniel, do.	-	5th May,	1815	4	48	Widow intermarried, July 6, 1816.

B—Continued.

KENTUCKY—Continued.

No.	Names of decedents, &c.	Rank or grade.	Original commencement of pension.	Pension per month.	Pension per annum.	Remarks, &c.
1068	Smith, William, *widow*	Private	22d Jan. 1813	$4 00	$48 00	
1069	Shingleton, Wm., do.	-	22d Jan. -	4	48	
1070	Scott, Abraham, *children*	-	1st March, -	4	48	
1071	Shoomate, Benj'n do.	-	11th Sept. -	4	48	
1072	Samples, Samuel, *widow*	-	22d Jan. -	4	48	
1073	Shelton, William, do.	-	6th March, 1815	4	48	
1074	Sproul, Alexander, do.	-	20th Nov. 1813	4	48	
1075	Straton, John, do.	-	5th May, -	4	48	
1076	Stepp, William, do.	-	21st Feb. 1815	4	48	
1077	Snediger, Moses, do.	-	28th March,1814	4	48	
1078	Swim, Alexander, do.	-	10th May, -	4	48	
1079	Shepherd, John, do.	-	30th March, -	4	48	
1080	Smith, John, do.	-	9th Feb. 1813	4	48	
1081	Skidmore, William, do.	-	24th Sept. -	4	48	
1082	See, William, do.	-	25th Oct. -	4	48	

B—Continued.

KENTUCKY—Continued.

No.	Names of decedents, &c.	Rank or grade.	Original commencement of pension.		Pension per month.		Pension per annum.		Remarks, &c.
1083	Shoemaker, Thos. *widow*	Private	1st Jan.	1814	$4	00	$48	00	See act of March 3d, 1817.
1084	Stevens, Thomas, do.	-	15th Dec.	1812	4		48		
1085	Seller, Jonathan, do.	-	22d Jan.	1813	4		48		Do. do. do.
1086	Stapp, Wiatt, do.	-	25th Sept.	1812	4		48		Do. do. do.
1087	Shryock, Christian, do.	-	5th Nov.	-	4		48		
1088	Throckmorton, Saml. do.	-	22d Jan.	1813	4		48		
1089	Tutt, Lewis Yauncy, do.	-	22d Jan.	1813	4		48		
1090	Taylor, Henry, do.	-	15th May,	-	4		48		
1091	Tate, John, do.	Sergeant	22d Jan.	-	5	50	66		
1092	Turner, Pleasant, do.	Private	5th May,	-	4		48		
1093	Trotter, James, do.	-	31st Oct.	-	4		48		
1094	Tanner, John, do.	-	11th Nov.	-	4		48		
1095	Thacker, Elijah, do.	-	3d April,	-	4		48		
1096	Trueman, Andrew, do.	-	17th Dec.	1814	4		48		

B.—Continued.

KENTUCKY—*Continued*

No.	Names of decedents, &c.	Rank or grade.	Original commencement of pension.	Pension per month.	Pension per annum.	Remarks, &c.
1097	Uselton, William, *widow*	Private	15th March, 1814	$ 4 00	$ 48 00	
1098	Vanlandingham, George *widow*					
1099	Vancleave, Benj'n *widow*	-	11th Feb. -	4	48	
1100	Wilson, James, do.	-	32d Jan. 1813	4	48	
1101	Whetley, William, do.	-	22d Jan. -	4	48	
1102	Wright, Nathaniel, do.	-	5th Oct. -	4	48	
1103	Wiley, Benjamin, do.	-	27th May, -	4	48	
1104	Williamson, John, do.	-	18th Feb. 1815	4	48	
			3d Nov. 1812	4	48	See act of March 3d, 1817.
1105	Wheeler, Thomas, do.	Sergeant	5th May, 1813	5 50	66	
1106	Whitaker, Aquilla, do.	Private	22d Jan. -	4	48	
1107	Walker, William, do.	Major	7th March, -	25	300	
1108	Williams, Bazel, do.	Private	25th Dec. 1813	4	48	
1109	Wills, David, do.	-	27th Nov. -	4	48	

B—Continued.

KENTUCKY—Continued.

No.	Names of decedents, &c.	Rank or grade.	Original commencement of pension.	Pension per month.	Pension per annum.	Remarks, &c.
1110	Williams, John, *widow*	Private	16th Jan. 1813	$ 4 00	$ 48 00	
1111	Wiley, James, do.	-	31st Dec. -	4	48	
1112	Williams, David, do.	-	3d July, -	4	48	
1113	Wetherford, Elijah, do.	-	22d Jan. -	4	48	
1114	Welch, Thomas B. do.	-	5th May, -	4	48	
1115	Whitmore, Abraham, do.	-	5th May, -	4	48	
1116	Williams, John, do.	1st lieutenant	22d Jan. -	15	180	
1117	Young, Alexander, do.	Private	5th May, -	4	48	
1118	Yates, James, do.	-	29th Dec. 1814	4	48	
1119	York, Aquilla, do.	-	4th Aug. 1813	4	48	
					$21,036 96	

B—Continued.

OHIO.

No.	Names of decedents, &c.	Rank or grade.	Original commencement of pension.	Pension per month.	Pension per annum.	Remarks, &c.
1120	Anderson, Wm. *widow*	Private	22d Nov. 1813	$4	$48 00	
1121	Allebaugh, John, do.	-	27th Sept. -	4	48	
1122	Asbel, Robert, do.	-	25th Dec. -	4	48	
1123	Boulebough, Abraham, *widow and children*	-	28th Feb. 1814	4	48	Widow intermarried, Oct. 15, 1814.
1124	Ball, Isaiah, *widow*	-	1st Jan. -	4	48	Do. do. 3d Aug. 1815.
1125	Beason, James, do.	-	7th April, -	4	48	Do. do. 17th Oct 1815.
1126	Briney, Frederick, do.	-	29th July, 1813	4	48	
1127	Bryant, John, do.	-	20th July, -	4	48	
1128	Bigham, Alexander do.	-	20th July, -	4	48	
1129	Brown, Clayton, do.	-	9th Nov. -	4	48	
1130	Baldwin, Caleb, *widow and child*	1st lieutenant	9th March, -	15	180	Do. do. 5th June, 1816.
1131	Britton, Apollo, *widow*	Private	20th Dec. -	4	48	

B—Continued.

OHIO—Continued.

No.	Names of decedents, &c.	Rank or grade.	Original commencement of pension	Pension per month.	Pension per annum.	Remarks, &c.
1132	Beans, Moses, *widow and children*	Private	16th Dec. 1813	$ 4 00	$ 48 00	Widow intermarried 14th Aug. 1815.
1133	Berryman, John, *widow*	-	17th Nov. -	4	48	See act of March 3d, 1817.
1134	Borden, George, do.	-	14th July, 1812	4	48	
1135	Boots, George, do.	Corporal	22d Nov. -	3 66	43 92	
1136	Baily, Thomas Z. do.	Private	29th July, 1813	4	48	Widow intermarried 30th Nov. 1815.
1137	Brosier, Peter, do.	-	24th Aug. -	4	48	
1138	Boatman, George, do.	-	5th April. 1814	4	48	Do. du. 18th Jan.1817.
1139	Bowman, Gilbert, do.	-	8th Nov. 1813	4	48	
1140	Brandlebury, Jacob, do.	-	23d Feb. -	4	48	
1141	Boerstler, Jacob, do.	Captain	5th Aug. 1812	20	240	
1142	Clark, Stephanes, do.	Corporal	23d March, 1814	5	60	

B—Continued.

OHIO—Continued.

No.	Names of decedents, &c.	Rank or grade.	Original commencement of pension.	Pension per month.	Pension per annum.	Remarks, &c.
1143	Cooksey, Josiah, *widow and children*	Private	5th Aug. 1813	$4 00	$ 48 00	Widow intermarried, May 27, 1815.
1144	Chance, William, *widow*	-	10th Dec. -	4	48	
1145	Colby, Samuel, *widow and children*	-	21st May, -	4	48	Do. do. 23d June, 1814.
1146	Carpenter, Joseph, *widow*	Captain	20th Feb. 1814	20	240	
1147	Cassin, Thomas, do.	Private	30th Sept. -	4	48	
1148	Cushing, Daniel, do.	Captain	24th March, 1815	20	240	
1149	Cochran, Andrew, do	Private	20th Feb. 1814	4	48	
1150	Campton, Robert, *widow and children*	-	5th Aug. 1812	4	48	Widow intermarried April 7, 181-, eal- so act of March 3d, 1817.
1151	Campbell, Andrew *widow*	-	4th April, 1814	4	48	

B—Continued.

OHIO—Continued.

No.	Names of decedents, &c.	Rank or grade.	Original commencement of pension.	Pension per month.	Pension per annum.	Remarks, &c.
1152	Craig, John, *widow*	Private	7th Aug. 1813	$4 00	$48 00	See act of March 3d, 1817.
1153	Clark, Isaac, do	-	15th Sept. 1812	4	48	
1154	Culp, Jacob, do.	-	5th March, 1813	4	48	
1155	Carmene, Blades, *widow and children*	-	31st Dec. -	4	48	Widow intermarried, 1st Jan. 1815.
1156	Douthit, Jacob, *widow*	-	9th Oct. -	4	48	
1157	Deibler, George, do.	-	24th Sept. 1812	4	48	See act of March 3d, 1817.
1158	Devore, Nathan, do.	Corporal	7th Dec. -	3 66	43 92	
1159	Doty, William, *widow and children*	Private	14th Nov. 1813	4	48	
1160	Lewis, *widon*	Sergeant	26th Aug. 1812	4	48·	
1161	Dever, Benjamin, do.	Private	5th Aug. -	4	48	Do. do. do. do.

B—Continued.

OHIO—Continued.

No.	Names of decedents, &c.	Rank or grade.	Original commencement of pension.	Pension per month.	Pension per annum.	Remarks, &c.
1162	Danford, William, *widow*	Private	23d Oct. 1813	$4 00	$48 00	
1163	Dollashide, Wm. do.	-	15th May, -	4	48	See act of March 3d, 1817.
1164	Deuton. Jonathan, do.	-	22d Nov. 1812	4	48	Do. do. do. do.
1165	Denny, David, do.	-	4th Sept. -	4	48	
1166	Davis, William, do.	-	21st May, 1813	4	48	
1167	Edwards, Josias, do.	Ensign	23d March, 1814	10	120	
1168	Farner, Michael M. d.	Private	9th Sept. 1813	4	48	
1169	Fulk, Peter, *widow and child*	-	23d May, 1814	4	48	Widow intermarried, June 13, 1815.
1170	Ford, William, *widow*	-	7th July, 1813	4	48	
1171	Foreman, Isaac, do.	-	25th March, -	4	48	Do. do. 21st March. 1816.
1172	Frees, Adam, do.	-	10th June, -	4	48	

B—Continued.

OHIO—Continued.

No.	Names of decedents, &c.	Rank or grade.	Original commencement of pension.	Pension per month.	Pension per annum.	Remarks, &c.
1173	Flynn, Hugh, *widow and children*	Captain	15th Aug. 1813	$ 20 00	$240 00	Widow died May 9, 1814.
1174	Gaston, John, *widow*	-	16th Nov. 1812	20	240	See act of March 3, 1817.
1175	Grey, Mathew, do.	Private	8th Sept. -	4	48	
1176	Griffith, James, do.	Sergeant	7th Nov. 1813	5 50	66	
1177	Guntridge, John, do.	Private	9th Sept.	4	48	
1178	Gee, William, do.	-	1st Jan. 1814	4	48	
1179	Gillaspy, Thomas, do.	-	14th Feb. -	4	48	
1180	Garrison, Jesse, do.	-	4th Jan. -	4	48	
1181	Green, Charles, do.	-	17th Oct. 1813	4	48	
1182	Gilchrist, Robert, do.	Captain	5th Aug. 1812	20	240	
1183	Harr, Isaiah, do.	Corporal	1th May, 1813	5	60	
1184	Holston, William, do.	Private	23d Dec. 1814	4	48	

B—Continued.

OHIO—Continued.

No.	Names of decedents, &c.	Rank or grade.	Original commencement of pension.	Pension per month.	Pension per annum.	Remarks, &c.
1185	Hale, Samuel, *widow*	Private	1st Nov. 1813	$4 00	$48 00	Widow intermarried, 30th Nov. 1815.
1186	Hammett, Joseph, do.	-	5th Jan. 1814	4	48	
1187	Hollow, Philip, do.	-	5th Nov. 1813	4	48	
1188	Holt, James, do.	-	1st Sept. -	4	48	
1189	Hall, John, do.	-	1st Dec. 1814	4	48	
1190	Ice, John	do.	12th Feb. -	4	48	Do. do. July 30, 1816.
1191	Johnson, William, do.	-	6th Aug.	4	48	
1192	Jacob, Gilson, do.	-	1st Sept. 1813	4	48	Widow intermarried, July 30, 1813. (See also act of March 3, 1817
1193	Johnson, Thomas, do.	-	9th Aug. 1812	4	48	
1194	Jacobs, Jacob, *widow and children*	1st lieutenant	14th April, 1813	15	180	Widow intermarried, 1st May, 1815.

B—Continued.

OHIO—Continued.

No.	Names of decedents, &c.	Rank or grade.	Original commencement of pension.	Pension per month.	Pension per annum.	Remarks, &c.
1195	Jackson, Gideon, *widow*	Corporal	5th Aug. 1812	$ 3 66	$ 43 92	
1196	King, Robert, do.	Private	3d May, 1815	4	48	
1197	Kincaid, Samuel, do.	-	5th May, -	4	48	
1198	Kirkpatrick, Charles, *widow and children*	-	20th Sept. 1812	4	48	Widow intermarried, Aug. 19, 1813. (See also act of March 3, 1817.)
1199	Kilgour, William, *widow*	Captain	14th April, 1814	20	240	
1200	King, John, do.	Private	6th Oct. -	4	48	
1201	Kerr, William, do.	-	28th Feb. -	4	48	
1202	Kirk, George, do.	-	22d April, -	4	48	
1203	Kestor, Paul, do.	-	10th April, -	4	48	
1204	Lemunyan, Stephen, do.	-	21st April, -	4	48	
1205	Linton, William, do.	-	5th April, -	4	48	Do. do. Feb. 27, 1816.
1206	Litle, Robert, do.	Corporal	8th Sept. 1818	5	60	

B—Continued.

OHIO—Continued.

No.	Names of decedents, &c.	Rank or grade.	Original commencement of pension.	Pension per month.	Pension per annum.	Remarks, &c.
1207	Lampson, Eleazer, *widow and child*	Private	4th Dec. 1812	$ 4 00	$48 00	Widow intermarried March 15, 1815. (See also act March 3, 1817.
1208	Lamont, Robert, *widow*	-	2d Feb. 1813	4	48	Do. do. Aug. 2, 1815.
1209	Lancaster, Wm. do.	-	1st June, -	4	48	
1210	Leforce, Robinson, do.	-	4th March, -	4	48	
1211	Moses, Thomas, do.	-	16th March, 1814	4	48	Widow intermarried, Nov. 16, 1816.
1212	Mullin, William, do.	Sergeant	12th Jan. -	5 50	66	
1213	Mitten, Isaias, do.	Private	1st Feb. -	4	48	Do. do. Oct. 28, 1816.
1214	M'Bride, John, do.	-	4th April, -	4	48	
1215	Millikan, John, *widow and children*	1st Lieutenant	25th March, -	15	180	Do. do. June 8, -
1216	M'Knight, John C. *widow*	Private	4th Nov. 1813	4	48	
1217	M'Clurg, David, do.	-	1st Nov. -	4	48	Do. do. April 1, 1816.

B—Continued.

OHIO—Continued.

No.	Names of decedents, &c.	Rank or grade.	Original commencement of pension.	Pension per month.	Pension per annum.	Remarks, &c.
1218	M'Fall, Malcom, *widow*	Private	6th Nov. 1812	$4 00	$48 00	See act of March 3d, 1817.
1219	Murphy, Samuel, do.	-	4th Sept. -	4	43	Do. do. do. do.
1220	Meeker, Peter, do.	-	7th May, 1814	4	48	
1221	M'Dill, or Madill, Thomas, *widow*	-	13th June, 1813	4	48	
1222	M'Neal, Samuel, *widow*	Sergeant	10th Jan. 1814	4	48	
1223	Michael, Paul, do.	Private	26th Nov. 1813	5 50	66	
1224	Mount, John, do.	-	27th Oct. -	4	48	
1225	Musterson, Jeremiah, do.	-	28th Dec. -	4	48	
1226	Miller, Isaac, do.	Sergeant	1st Oct. -	5 50	66	
1227	M'Cune, Thomas, do.	Corporal	26th March, 1814	5	60	
1228	M'Pherson, John, do.	Private	11th Nov. 1813	4	48	
1229	Mathers, Daniel, do.	-	20th Aug. -	4	48	
1230	Mingers, Calvin, *widow and children*	-	13th Nov. -	4	48	{ Widow intermarried, Aug. 18, 1814,

B—Continued.

OHIO—Continued.

No.	Names of decedents, &c.	Rank or grade.	Original commencement of pension.	Pension per month.	Pension per annum.	Remarks, &c.
1231	Moore, Thomas, *widow*	Private	16th Dec. 1813	$4 00	$ 48 00	
1232	Moreland, John, do.	-	29th Sept. 1813	4	48	
1233	Mershon, Solomon, *widow and children*	-	29th Oct. 1814	4	48	Widow intermarried, Jan. 24, 1816.
1234	McConnell, William, *widow and children*	-	25th July, 1812	4	48	Do. do. April 16, 1815. (See also act of 3d March, 1817.)
1235	Miller, John, *widow*	-	13th Nov. 1813	4	48	
1236	Mathews, John, do.	-	3d March, 1814	4	48	Do. do. Aug. 4, 1816.
1237	Meek, William, do.	-	23d Feb. 1813	4	48	
1238	M'Aliste, Samuel, do.	-	1st Sept. 1812	4	48	Do. do. 2d May, 1816. (See also act of 3d March, 1817.)
1239	M'Coy, Angus, do.	1st lieutenant	13th Aug. 1813	15	180	

B—Continued.

OHIO—Continued.

No.	Names of decedents, &c.	Rank or grade.	Original commencement of pension.	Pension per month.	Pension per annum.	Remarks, &c.
1240	Nealy, John, *widow*	Private	15th June, 1813	$4 00	$ 48 00	Widow intermarried, May 24, 1815.
1241	Nash, John, do.	-	26th Dec. -	4	48	See act of March 3d, 1817.
1242	Owen, Abraham, do.	Aid de camp	7th Nov. 1811	25	300	
1243	Parks, George, do.	Private	28th Nov. -	4	48	
1244	Plowman, Mesheck, do.	Sergeant	3d Aug. 1812	4	48	
1245	Porter, James, do.	Private	17th Nov 1813	4	48	
1246	Powers, Avery, do.	-	25th July, 1812	4	48	See act of March 3d, 1817.
1247	Phillips, Enoch, do.	-	18th Nov. 1813	4	48	Widow intermarried, 24th, Oct. 1815.
1248	Pierce, Benoni, do.	Captain	18th Dec. 1812	20	240	
1249	Randolph, Henry, *widow and children*	Private	12th Dec. 1813	4	48	Do.do. 18th Mar. 1815
1250	Reynolds, Lightm, *widow*	-	4th Dec. -	4	48	

41

B—Continued.

OHIO—Continued.

No.	Names of decedents, &c.	Rank or grade.	Original commencement of pension.	Pension per month.	Pension per annum.	Remarks, &c.
1251	Ramsey, Nathan, *widow*	Private	7th Dec. 1812	$4 00	$ 48 00	See act of March 3d, 1817.
1252	Roath, Joseph, do.	-	13th June, 1814	4	48	
1253	Ross, Adam, do.	-	30th April, 1813	4	48	
1254	Ramsey, John, do.	1st lieutenant	21st March, -	15	180	
1255	Russell, Jeremiah, do.	Private	5th Nov. -	4	48	
1256	Reed, Benjamin, do.	-	22d Jan. -	4	48	
1257	Reeves, James, do.	-	27th Nov. -	4	48	Widow intermarried 14th Aug. 1817.
1258	Rambo, Tobias, do.	-	8th Jan. -	4	48	
1259	Reppy, Joseph, do.	-	15th March, -	4	48	See act of 10th April, 1812.
1260	Randolph, Thomas, do.	-	7th Nov. 1811	3 33	39 96	
1261	Sturgeon, Robert, do.	•	4th Dec. 1813	4	48	Widow intermarried, June 4, 1816.

B—Continued.

OHIO—Continued.

No.	Names of decedents, &c.	Rank or grade.	Original commencement of pension.	Pension per month.	Pension per annum.	Remarks, &c.
1262	Spurling, Jesse, *widow*	Private	13th July, 1813	S 4 00	$ 48 00	
1263	Snider, Arrold, *widow and children*	-	22d June, -	4	48	Widow intermarried 6th Dec. 1815.
1264	Stout, George W. *widow*	Musician	5th Oct. -	4 50	54	
1265	Salvister, James, do.	Private	24th Oct. -	4	48	
1266	Shaw, Freeman, do.	-	30th April, -	4	48	
1267	Smith, Henry, do.	Sergeant	3d Jan. 1814	5 50	66	Widow intermarried, 17th Aug. 1815.
1268	Stewart, Edie, do.	Private	15th Feb. - 1815	4	48	
1269	Spence, Peter, do.	-	2d Sept. 1815	4	48	
1270	Strickland, Henry, do.	-	26th Dec. 1813	4	48	
1271	Study-baker, John, do.	-	3d Oct. -	4	48	
1272	Skeels, Henry, do.	-	2d Dec. -	4	48	
1273	Shaw, Samuel, do.	Qr. Master	13th Aug. -	5	60	

B—Continued.

OHIO—Continued.

No.	Names of decedents, &c.	Rank or grade.	Original commencement of pension.	Pension per month.	Pension per annum.	Remarks, &c.
1274	Topping Zophar, *widow*	Private	27th Sept. 1814	$ 4 00	$ 48	Widow intermarried Aug. 8, 1816.
1275	Traverse, Wm. do.	-	27th June, 1815	4	48	
1276	Thompson, Archibald, do.	Sergeant	18th April, 1814	5 50	66	Do. do. March 1, 1815.
1277	Taff, Abraham, do.	Private	7th Jan. -	4	48	
1278	Thomas, Arthur, do.	Captain	1st Sept. 1813	20	£40	
1279	Trovinger, Jacob, do.	Private	13th Dec. -	4	48	
1280	Ulery, Henry, do.	Captain	5th Aug. 1812	20	240	
1281	Van Camp, Moses. do.	Private	14th Dec. 1813	4	48	
1282	Van Vickle, Robt. do.	-	2d July, -	4	48	Do. do. Aug. 15, 1816.
1283	Warden, Benj. do.	Fifer	1st May, 1814	4 50	54	
1284	Wilkins, Cornelius, do.	Private	3d May, 1813	4	48	Do. do. March 2, 1815.
1285	Wright, Samuel, do.	-	18th Feb. -	4	48	
1286	Wright, Robert B. *widow and children*	-	9th May, 1814	4	48	Do. do. April 21, 1816

B.—Continued.

OHIO—Continued.

No.	Names of decedents, &c.	Rank or grade.	Original commencement of pension.	Pension per month.	Pension per annum.	Remarks, &c.
1287	Wirick, Jacob, *widow and children*	Drummer	12th Dec. 1812	$ 3 66	$ 43 92	Widow intermarried Nov. 21, 1814.
1288	Warnick, Robert, *widow*	Private	15th Sept. -	4	48	See act of March 3d, 1817.
1289	Woods, Charles, do.	-	25th Nov. 1813	4	48	
1290	Wilson, Sylvester, do.	-	13th July, -	4	48	
1291	Warman, Joshua, *widow and children*	Corporal	6th March, -	5	60	
1292	Watts, Henry, *widow*	Private	22d Dec. -	4	48	Widow intermarried 12th Feb. 1815.
1293	Wilson, Thomas, do.	-	9th Dec. -	4	48	
1294	Wells, Joseph, do.	-	30th Oct. -	4	48	
1295	Wells, Charles, do.	-	11th Dec. -	4	48	
1296	Wilson, Peter, do.	-	9th Sept. 1814	4	48	

B—Continued.

OHIO—Continued.

No.	Names of decedents, &c.	Rank or grade.	Original commencement of pension.	Pension per month.	Pension per annum.	Remarks, &c.
1297	Walker, Isaac, *widow*	Captain	5th April, 1813	$20 00	$ 240 00	
1298	Willis, William, do.	Private	1st April, 1814	4	48	
1299	Wright, William, do.	-	29th Aug. 1813	4	48	
1300	Yatman, Peter, do.	-	5th Dec. -	4	48	
					$ 11,951 64	

B—Continued.

TENNESSEE.

No.	Names of decedents, &c.	Rank or grade.	Original commencement of pension.	Pension per month.	Pension per annum.	Remarks, &c.
1201	Anderson, John, *widow and children*	Lieut. Colonel	27th Oct. 1814	$ 30 00	$ 360 00	Widow intermarried 25th April, 1816.
1302	Anthony, Wm. B. *widow*	Private	28th Dec. -	4	48	
1303	Arnel, William, do.	-	16th Feb. -	4	48	
1304	Adams, Howell, do.	2d lieutenant	28th Jan. -	12 50	150	
1305	Archer, Thomas, do.	Private	12th March, 1815	4	48	
1306	Anderson, Eleanor, do.	-	14th Jan. -	4	48	
1307	Allen, James, do.	-	6th Jan. -	4	48	
1308	Arant, Harris, do.	3d lieutenant	12th Sept. 1814	4	48	
1309	Aken, Harrison, do.	-	11th Feb. 1815	11 50	138	
1310	Allen, John, do.	Private	14th March, -	4	48	
1311	Adams, Peter, do.	-	19th March, 1814	4	48	
1312	Berry, James, do.	1st lieutenant	27th March, -	15	180	
1313	Bean, William, do.	Private	14th Jan. 1815	4	48	

B—Continued.

TENNESSEE—Continued.

No.	Names of decedents, &c.	Rank or grade.	Original commencement of pension.		Pension per month.	Pension per annum.	Remarks, &c.
1314	Britten, Cornelius, *widow*	Private	1st May,	1815	$4 00	$ 48 00	
1315	Bitner, Samuel,	do.	19th Nov.	1814	4	48	
1316	Barton, Samuel,	1st lieutenant	9th Nov.	1813	15	180	
1317	Brewer, John,	Private	3d April,	1815	4	48	
1318	Byrns, James,	-	14th Feb.	-	4	48	
1319	Belt, Middleton,	-	4th Feb.	-	4	48	
1320	Boothe, Samuel,	-	1st Jan.	-	4	48	
1321	Barnet, Samuel,	-	20th March,	-	4	48	
1322	Blair, Joseph,	-	8th Jan.	-	4	48	
1323	ond, Thomas,	-	9th Feb.	1814	4	48	
1324	Branden, John,	-	8th Dec.	-	4	48	
1325	Barefoot, Jonathan,	do.	10th Dec.	-	4	48	
1326	Burrs, Robert,	do.	2d Nov.	1813	4	60	
1327	ason, John,	do.	22d Jan.	1814	5	60	
1328	Baley, John,	do.	3d Nov.	1813	5	60	

B—Continued.

TENNESSEE—Continued.

No.	Names of decedents, &c.	Rank or grade.	Original commencement of pension.	Pension per month.	Pension per annum.	Remarks, &c.
1329	Bullard, Joseph, *widow*	Private	10th Feb. 1815	$4	$48 00	
1330	Burnes, James, do.	-	14th April, -	4	48	
1331	Brinckley, Samuel, do.	-	8th March, -	4	48	
1332	Bogle, Thomas, do.	-	10th Jan. -	4	48	
1333	Croff, Jacob, do.	-	2d Dec. 1814	4	48	Widow intermarried, 14th May, 1816.
1334	Collins, John, do.	-	11th Feb. 1815	4	48	
1335	Caitharp, James, do.	-	27th Feb. -	4	48	
1336	Covington, Henry, do.	-	11th March, -	4	48	
1337	Clark, Richard, do.	-	14th Feb. -	4	48	
1338	Crumley, Jacob, do.	-	28th April, 1814	4	48	
1339	Craig, William, do.	-	26th Jan. 1815	4	48	
1340	Clark, William C. do.	-	31st Jan. 1813	4	48	
1341	Cathca., Joseph, do.	-	3d April, 1814	4	48	
1342	Cooper, Absolam, do.	-	22d Feb. -	4	48	

B—Continued.

TENNESSEE—Continued.

No.	Names of decedents, &c.	Rank or grade.	Original commencement of pension.	Pension per month.	Pension per annum.	Remarks, &c.
1343	Carson, Samuel, *widow*	Private	16th March, 1815.	$4 00	$48 00	
1344	Cosby, James, do.	-	26th March, -	4	48	
1345	Compton, Thomas, do.	-	10th April, -	4	48	
1346	Clark, James, do.	-	13th Nov. 1814	4	48	
1347	Childress, James, do.	-	12th March, 1815	4	48	
1348	Carson, Willis, do.	Corporal	23d Feb. -	5	60	
1349	Coleburn, Richard, do.	Private	8th March, -	4	48	
1350	Chandler, Thomas, do.	-	6th April, 1814	4	48	
1351	Claxton, James, do.	-	11th Feb. 1815	4	48	
1352	Clark, Benjamin M. *widow and children*	-	11th Nov. 1814	4	48	Widow intermarried, Feb. 1, 1816.
1353	Crews, Edward, *widow*	-	22d Dec. -	4	48	
1354	Dossett, Willis, do.	-	3d Nov. 1813.	4	48	

B—Continued.

TENNESSEE—Continued.

No.	Names of decedents, &c.	Rank or grade.	Original com-n-mencement of pension.	Pension per month.	Pension per annum.	Remarks, &c.
1355	Diddle, John, *widow*	Private	18th March, 1814	$4 00	$48 00	
1356	Daniel, James, do.	-	22d April, 1815	4	48	
1357	Delany, John, do.	-	15th Feb. -	4	48	
1358	Dudney, Abraham, do.	Captain	29th Nov. -	20	240	
1359	Darnall, Benjamin, do.	Trumpeter	13th March, 1813	4 50	54	
1360	Dixon, Robert, do.	Private	9th Feb. 1815	4	48	
1361	Dean, Luke H. do.	Corporal	26th Oct. 1813	5	60	Widow intermarried, 2d April, 1817.
1362	Doak, John, do.	Captain	16th Feb. 1815	20	240	
1363	Davidson, William, do.	Private	20th March, -	4	48	
1364	Dickson, Edmond, do.	-	31st Jan. -	4	48	
1365	Downey, or Draney, John, *widow*	-	28th March, -	4	48	
1366	Duncan, Charles, *widow*	-	22d Feb. -	4	48	
1367	Darr, Henry, do.	-	22d Jan. 1814	4	48	

B—Continued.

TENNESSEE—Continued.

No.	Names of decedents, &c.	Rank or grade.	Original commencement of pension.	Pension per month.	Pension per annum.	Remarks, &c.
1368	Edwards, Andrew, *widow*	Private	12th March, 1814	$4 00	$ 48 00	
1369	Eakin, Jesse, do.	-	16th Feb. 1815	4	48	
1370	Ellis, Simeon, do.	-	27th March, 1814	4	48	
1371	Estis, Gallant, do.	-	26th Jan. -	4	48	
1372	Edington, Luke F. do.	Sergeant	23d Dec. -	5 50	66	
1373	Edgeor Age, Moses, do.	Private	23d Feb. 1815	4	48	
1374	Ellitt or Elliott, Wm. do.	-	22d Jan. -	4	48	
1375	Eakins, David, do.	-	24th Jan. 1814	4	48	
1376	Eagins, William, do.	2d lieutenant	22d Jan. -	12 50	150	
1377	Eatherage, Merrett, do.	Private	1st May, -	4	48	
1378	Farr, John, do.	-	27th Oct. 1815	4	48	
1379	Farmer, James, do.	-	23d Feb. 1815	4	48	
1380	Franks, Elijah, do.	Corporal	7th Feb. -	5	60	Widow intermarried, 20th Aug. 1815.
1381	Fuller, Henry, do.	Private	4th April, 1814	4	48	
1382	Forrester, Jonathan, do.	Musician	22d Feb. 1815	4 50	54	

B—Continued.

TENNESSEE—Continued.

No.	Names of decedents, &c.	Rank or grade.	Original commencement of pension.		Pension per month.	Pension per annum.	Remarks, &c.
1383	Fann, Elijah, *widow*	Private	1st Dec.	1813	$4 00	$48 00	
1384	Forrest, Isaac, do.	-	7th Feb.	1815	4	48	
1385	Farley, Jesse, do.	1st lieutenant	22d April,	-	15	180	
1386	Feeland, or Fielding, William, *widow*	Private	9th Feb.	-	4	48	
1387	Forrester, Charles, do.	-	23d Dec.	1814	4	48	Widow intermarried, 15th June, 1815.
1388	Foster, Davies, do.	-	15th Oct.	1813	4	48	
1389	Felton, William, do.	-	7th Dec.	-	4	48	
1390	Furgerson, Samuel, do.	-	28th Jan.	1815	4	48	
1391	Frost, Alexander, do.	-	30th Dec.	1814	4	48	
1392	Forsythe, Benjamin, do.	Lieut. colonel	28th June,	-	30	360	
1393	Goin, Noah, or Gowan Menoah, *widow*	Corporal	22d April,	1815	5	60	
1394	Grayham, James, do.	Private	1st Nov.	1814	4	48	

B—Continued.

TENNESSEE—Continued.

No.	Names of decedents, &c.	Rank or grade.	Original commencement of pension.	Pension per month.	Pension per annum.	Remarks, &c.
1395	Gibbs, Nicholas, *widow*	Captain	27th March, 1814	$20 00	$240 00	
1396	Goard, Isham, do.	Private	14th Jan. 1815	4	48	
1397	Gardiner, Robert, do.	-	5th Jan. -	4	48	
1398	Gibson, John, do.	-	25th Jan. -	4	48	
1399	Gower, William, E. do.	-	16th Jan. -	4	48	
1400	Garrett, Catlett, do.	-	21st Nov. 1814	4	48	
1401	Gower, Alexander K. *widow*	Sergeant	25th March, 1815	5 50	66	
1402	Gardiner, Josiah, *widow*	Private	1st June, 1814	4	48	
1403	Guess, William, do.	-	20th Jan. 1813	4	48	
1404	Going, Andrew, do.	-	30th Jan. 1815	4	48	
1405	Gibson, Joseph, do.	-	30th Dec. 1814	4	48	
1406	Honn, George, do.	Corporal	26th March, 1815	5	66	
1407	Hamilton, John, do.	Private	13th Feb. -	4	48	
1408	Henderson, James, do.	Lieut. colonel	28th Dec. 1814	30	360	

B—Continued.

TENNESSEE—Continued.

No.	Names of decedents, &c.	Rank or grade.	Original commencement of pension.	Pension per month.	Pension per annum.	Remarks, &c.
1409	Hitchcock, Elijah, *widow*	Private	27th Dec. 1813	$ 4 00	$ 48 00	
1410	Hancock, Clement, do.	Sergeant	8th Jan. 1815	5 50	66	
1411	Hicks, Peter, do.	Private	1st Jan. -	4	48	
1412	Headrick, Joseph, do.	-	14th April, -	4	48	
1413	Harris, John, do.	Sergeant	17th March, -	5 50	66	
1414	Hopkins, John, do.	Private	12th Dec. 1813	4	48	
1415	Hill, George, do.	-	28th April, 1815	4	48	
1416	Hunter, Aaron, do.	3d lieutenant	20th Feb. -	11 50	138	
1417	Helton, James, do.	Musician	15th Jan. -	4 50	54	Widow intermarried, 29th Jan. 1816.
1418	Henderson, Nathan, do.	Private	4th Feb. -	4	48	
1419	Hall, William, do.	" "	15th Feb. -	4	48	
1420	Hail, Thomas, do.	" "	1st Dec. 1813	4	48	
1421	Henry, John, do.	" "	28th Dec. 1814	4	48	
1422	Harris, Nathan, do.	"	9th Nov. 1813	4	48	

B—Continued.

TENNESSEE—Continued.

No.	Names of decedents, &c.	Rank or grade.	Original commencement of pension.	Pension per month.	Pension per annum.	Remarks, &c.
1423	Hall, Joseph, un. *widow*	Private	30th Sept. 1814	$ 4 00	$ 48 00	
1424	Hook, George do.	-	16th Nov. -	4	48	
1425	Hart, John, do.	-	18th Feb. 1815	4	48	
1426	Hoas, Albert, do.	Sergeant	6th Feb. -	5 50	66	
1427	Henby, or Henly, Joseph, *widow*	Private	13th March, -	4	48	
1428	Harris, John, *widow*	Corporal	12th Feb. -	5	60	
1429	Hite or Hight, John, do.	Private	16th Oct. 1814	4	48	
1430	Haun, John, do.	-	18th April, 1815	4	48	
1431	Hopper, John, do.	-	20th Feb. -	4	48	
1432	Hutton, John, do.	Sergeant	9th Nov. 1813	5 50	66	
1433	Harrison, Robert, do.	Private	15th Jan. 1815	4	48	
1434	Hudson, Thomas, B. do.	-	3d Nov. 1813	4	48	
1435	Hill, John, *widow and children*	Captain	22d Jan. 1814	20	240	Widow intermarried, 14th March, 1816.

B—Continued.

TENNESSEE—Continued.

No.	Names of decedents, &c.	Rank or grade.	Original commencement of pension.	Pension per month.	Pension per annum.	Remarks, &c.
1436	House, Green, *widow*	Private	13th Jan. 1813	$ 4 00	$48 00	
1437	Hutcherson, Josiah, do.	-	3d April, 1815	4	48	
1438	Hopper, Zachariah, do.	-	16th Nov. 1814	4	48	
1439	Howard, Richard, do.	-	2d Jan. 1815	4	48	
1440	Hutcherson, Reuben, do.	-	17th April, 1814	4	48	
1441	Jones, Isaac, do.	-	13th Jan. 1813	4	48	
1442	Jones, John, do.	-	1st Dec. -	4	48	
1443	Johnston, Thomas, do.	Sergeant	1st Dec. -	5 50	66	
1444	Jones, William, do.	Private	18th March, 1815	4	48	
1445	Jones, Daniel, do.	-	20th April, 1814	4	48	
1446	Jones, Reuben, do.	-	15th April, 1815	4	48	
1447	Jackson, Thomas, do.	Sergeant	25th April, -	5 50	66	
1448	Jenkins, Joseph, do.	-	20th Feb. -	5 50	66	
1449	Kelly, Daniel, do.	Private	27th March, 1814	4	48	
1450	Kerr, Wilson, do.	1st Lieutenant	24th Dec. -	15	180	

B—Continued.

TENNESSEE—Continued.

No.	Names of decedents, &c.	Rank or grade.	Original commencement of pension.		Pension per month.		Pension per annum.	Remarks, &c.
1451	Knox, William, *widow*	Private	24th Dec.	1813	$4	00	$48 00	
1452	Kavenaugh, James P. do.	1st lieutenant	5th April,	1815	15		180	
1453	Knight, James, do.	Private	20th Feb.	-	4		48	
1454	Knight, Robert, do.	-	22d Jan.	1814	4		48	
1455	Kidwell, Josiah, do.	-	14th Jan.	1815	4		48	
1456	Kerr, Alexander, do.	-	5th Jan.	-	4		48	
1457	Lomax, Thomas, do.	-	18th Nov.	1814	4		48	
1458	Longmire, William, do.	Corporal	20th Feb.	1815	5		60	
1459	Leamons, Wm. sen. do.	Sadler	23d Dec.	1814	6	50	78	
1460	Lislie, Seth, do.	Private	11th Dec.	-	4		48	
1461	Ligget, Daniel, do.	-	28th Feb.	1815	4		48	
1462	Lawson, Eppy, do.	2d lieutenant	21st April,	1814	12	50	150	
1463	Lambert, Aaron, do.	1st lieutenant	25th March,	-	15		180	
1464	Ledbetter, Lewis, do.	Private	1st Jan.	-	4		48	
1465	Little, James, do.	-	1st Nov.	-	4		48	

B—Continued.

TENNESSEE—*Continued.*

No.	Names of decedents, &c.	Rank or grade.	Original commencement of pension.		Pension per month.		Pension per annum.	Remarks, &c.
1466	Laws, Aaron, *widow*	Sergeant	2d Feb.	1815	$5	50	$66 00	
1467	Lewis, Hugh, do.	Private	14th Feb.	-	4		48	
1468	Latham, Vincent do.	-	15th Oct.	1814	4		48	
1469	M'Minn, William, do.	-	23d Dec.	-	4		48	
1470	Mallard, John, do.	Sergeant	28th Dec.	-	5	50	66	
1471	Merchant, David, do.	Private	20th Dec.	1813	4		48	
1472	Millard, George, do.	-	1st March,	1815	4		48	
1473	Myers, Jacob, do.	-	15th Jan.	-	4		48	
1474	Moore, James, do.	-	3d Nov.	1813	4		48	
1475	Miller, James, do.	-	21st Jan.	1815	4		48	
1476	Martin, Richard, do.	-	5th Feb.	-	4		48	
1477	Moore, John, do.	-	20th Dec.	1814	4		48	
1478	M'Neal, John, do.	Corporal	28th Nov.	-	5		60	
1479	Morris, Mathew, do.	Private	1st Feb.	-	4		48	
1480	Morrow, James, do.	-	5th Feb.	1815	4		48	

B—Continued.

TENNESSEE—Continued.

No.	Names of decedents, &c.	Rank or grade.	Original commencement of pension.	Pension per month.	Pension per annum.	Remarks, &c.
1481	M'Daniel, Joseph, *widow*	Private	8th Feb. 1815	$ 4 00	$ 48 00	
1482	Murray, Simeon, do.	.	8th Feb. -	4	48	
1483	M'Kinsey, Rolly, do.	.	10th Nov. 1813	4	48	
1484	M'Bride, Joseph, do.	.	14th May, 1815	4	48	
1485	Messelwhite, John, do.	.	8th June, 1815	4	48	
1486	Murphy, Ephraim, do.	.	16th Nov. 1813	4	48	
1487	M'Kee, Levin, do.	.	6th March, 1815	4	48	
1488	Moss, Benjamin, do.	.	27th Feb. -	4	48	
1489	Mathews, James, do.	.	9th Nov. 1813	4	48	
1490	Meek, James, do.	.	10th Feb. 1815	4	48	
1491	M'Minis, Joseph, do.	Sergeant	13th April, 1814	5 50	66	
1492	Morton, Thomas, do.	Private	20th March, 1815	4	48	
1493	Moore, Marchus, do.	Sergeant	23d Dec. 1814	5 50	66	
1494	Morgan, William, do.	Private	18th Oct. 1813	4	48	
1495	Macebyway,Daniel,do.	-	22d Nov -	4	48	

B.—Continued.

TENNESSEE—Continued.

No.	Names of decedents, &c.	Rank or grade.	Original commencement of pension.	Pension per month.	Pension per annum.	Remarks, &c.
1496	Mowl, Jacob, *widow*	Private	27th March, 1814	$ 4 00	$ 48 00	
1497	Morelock, George, do.	-	25th June, -	4	48	
1498	M'Ferson, Jonathan, do.	-	14th Feb. 1815	4	48	
1499	Morris, Hezekiah, do.	-	14th April, -	4	48	
1500	Moser, Christian, do.	-	13th March, -	4	48	
1501	Morrow, Daniel, do.	-	19th Nov. 1814	4	48	
1502	Myers, Frederick, do.	-	27th March, -	4	48	
1503	M'Donald, Joseph, do.	-	17th Feb. 1815	4	48	
1504	M'Adoo, John, *widow and children*	-	28th March, -	4	48	Widow intermarried 24th Oct. 1816.
1505	Meyers, William, *widow*	1st lieutenant	7th April, 1814	4	48	Do. do. Aug. 29, 1816.
1506	Moore, Robert, do.	-	9th Nov. 1813	15	180	
1506	Nichols, David, do.	Private	4th Feb. 1815	4	48	
1507	Norman, Ezekiel, do.	3d lieutenant	24th Sept. 1814	11 50	138	

B—Continued.

TENNESSEE—Continued.

No.	Names of decedents, &c.	Rank or grade.	Original commencement of pension.	Pension per month.	Pension per annum.	Remarks, &c.
1508	Nolen, Abraham, *widow*	Farrier	23d Dec. 1814	$6 50	$78 00	
1509	Northcut, John, do.	Private	20th Feb. 1815	4	48	
1510	Nunnery, Nathaniel, do.	-	22d March, -	4	48	
1511	Norris, James,	-	12th Feb. -	4	48	
1512	Noel, Riley, do.	-	5th March, -	4	48	
1513	Nance, Bird, do.	Captain	9th April, -	20	240	
1514	Nelson, Ambrose, do.	Private	22d Feb. -	4	48	
1515	Osborne, John, do.	-	24th Nov. 1813	4	48	
1516	Owens, William, do.	-	3d March, 1815	4	48	
1517	Oliver, Frederick, do.	-	17th April, -	4	48	
1518	Oneal, Jeremiah, do.	-	28th Dec. 1814	4	48	
1519	Owen, or Owens, Martin, *widow*	-	18th Jan. 1815	4	48	
1520	Oneal, William, *widow*	-	18th July, 1813	4	48	
1521	Privett, Mathew, do.	Corporal	24th Jan. -	5	60	

B—Continued.

TENNESSEE—Continued.

No.	Names of decedents, &c.	Rank or grade.	Original commencement of pension.		Pension per month.	Pension per annum.	Remarks, &c.
1522	Pace, James, *widow*	Captain	23d Dec.	1814	$20 00	$.240 00	
1523	Pace, John, do.	Private	9th Jan.	1815	4	48	
1524	Parker, Winbourn, do.	-	22d Feb.	-	4	48	
1525	Pybus, William, do.	-	6th Feb.	-	4	48	
1526	Paty, Jesse, do.	-	16th Feb.	-	4	48	
1527	Plant, William, do.	Corporl	1st March.	-	5	60	
1528	Parker, Nathan, do.	Private	1st April,	-	4	48	
1529	Phibbs, Richard, do.	-	28th Feb.	-	4	48	
1530	Perkins, Stephen, do.	-	21st March, 1814		4	48	
1531	Pankey, Riley, or W. R. *widow and children*	-	20th April,	-	4	48	Widow intermarried 1st July, 1817.
1532	Palton, James, *widow*	-	23d Nov.	1813	4	48	Do. do. 30th Nov. 1815.
1533	Perry, John, do.	-	16th Aug.	1814	4	48	
1534	Quarles, John B. do.	Captain	27th Jan.	-	20	240	

B—Continued.

TENNESSEE—Continued.

No.	Names of decedents, &c.		Rank or grade.	Original commencement of pension.	Pension per month.	Pension per annum.	Remarks, &c.
1535	Robinson, William, P.		Private	20th March, 1815	$4 00	$ 48 00	
	widow	widow		22d Feb. 1814	4	48	
1536	Roberts, John,	do.	-	13th April, -	4	48	
1537	Ruton, Enoch,	do.	-	8th Nov. -	4	48	
1538	Rice, Rowland,	do.	-	21st Feb. 1815	4	48	
1539	Rodgers, Jonathar,	do.	-	23d Feb. -	4	48	
1540	Reese, Caleb;	do.	-	17th Feb. -	4	48	
1541	Robinson, Daniel,	do.	-	14th Feb. -	4	48	
1542	Rodden, Jacob,	do.	-	19th Jan. -	4	48	
1543	Rhodes, William,	do.	-	23d Nov. 1813	4	48	
1544	Russell, Absolam,	do.	Captain	9th Nov. 1814	20	240	
1545	Robertson, John,	do.	Private	1st Feb. 1815	4	48	
1546	Reding, Lewis,	do.	-	6th Jan. -	4	48	
1547	Rogers, Elisha,	do.			4	48	Widow intermarried 9th April, 1816.
1548	Rose, Jacob,	do.	-	7th Sept. 1814	4	48	

B—Continued.

TENNESSEE—Continued.

No.	Names of decedents, &c.	Rank or grade.	Original commencement of pension.	Pension per month.	Pension per annum.	Remarks, &c.
1549	Rogers, Jesse, *widow*	Private	8th Jan. 1815	$4 00	$48 00	
1550	Relford, John, do.	-	19th Jan. -	4	48	
1551	Richardson, Fisher, do.	-	10th Feb. -	4	48	
1552	Ricketts, John, do.	-	15th April, -	4	48	
1553	Stockton, Marshall, do.	-	15th Dec. 1814	4	48	
1554	Stakes, William, do.	-	23d Feb. 1815	4	48	
1555	Sanders, David, do.	-	25th Feb. -	4	43	Widow intermarried 23d July, 1816.
1556	Smith. Bird, do.	Brig. general	19th Feb. -	52	624	
1557	Shankle, John, do.	Private	10th March, -	4	48	
1558	Spurlock, Harvey, do.	-	28th Jan. -	4	48	
1559	Sims, John, do.	-	16th April -	4	48	
1560	Smothers, James, do.	-	26th Aug. 1814	4	48	
1561	Stevens, Lorime, do.	-	21st Feb. 1815	4	43	
1562	Stafford, Samuel, do.	-	28th March, -	4	48	

44

B—Continued.

TENNESSEE—Continued.

No.	Names of decedents, &c.	Rank or grade.	Original commencement of pension.	Pension per month.	Pension per annum.	Remarks, &c.
1563	Sampson, Jesse, *widow*	Private	19th March, 1815	$4 00	$48 00	
1564	Srigley, Samuel, do.	Sergeant	27th Jan. -	5 50	66	
1565	Southall, James, do.	Private	16th Feb. -	4	48	
1566	Simpson, Gilbert, do.	"	3d Nov. 1813	4	48	
1567	Smith, Kinchen, do.	"	7th Jan. 1815	4	48	
1568	Sanders, James, do.	"	21st Feb. 1815	4	48	
1569	Shook, Abraham, do.	"	10th Dec. 1814	4	48	
1570	Skelleton, Joseph, do.	"	17th Feb. 1815	4	48	
1571	Smith, Edward, do.	3d lieutenant	23d Feb. -	11 50	138	
1572	Smalling, Soloman, do.	Private	22d Oct. 1814	4	48	
1573	Spragins, William, do.	"	15th Oct. 1814	4	48	
1574	Stubbs, Everett, do.	"	17th April, -	4	48	
1575	Shelton, George, do.	Ensign	26th Feb. 1815	10	120	
1576	Sugg, William, do.	Private	9th March, -	4	48	

B—Continued.

TENNESSEE—Continued.

No.	Names of decedents, &c.	Rank or grade.	Original commencement of pension.	Pension per month.	Pension per annum.	Remarks, &c.
1577	Simms, James, *widow*	Private	2d March, 1815	$4 00	$48 00	
1578	Short, Caleb, do.	2d lieutenant	7th March, -	12 50	150	
1579	Sumake, Andrew, do.	Private	2d Jan.	4	48	
1580	Savage, Kendall, do.	- -	17th Jan.	4	48	
1581	Sadler, Thomas, do.	- -	8th Feb.	4	48	
1582	Summers, Johnston, do.	- -	21st May, 1814	4	48	
1583	Smith, William, do.	- -	29th Jan. 1815	4	48	
1584	Stringer, Exekiel, *widow and children*	-	8th Feb. -	4	48	Widow intermarried, 6th Sept. 1815. Do. do. Nov. 7, 1816.
1585	Simmons, John, *widow*	- -	21st April, -	4	48	
1586	Smith, Jeremiah, do.	- -	22d Jan. 1814	4	48	
1587	Stone, John, do.	Cornet	6th Nov. 1813	10	120	
1588	Slaughter, Abraham, do.	Private	28th Dec. 1814	4	48	
1589	Speak, Thomas, do.	-	1st Dec. 1814	4	48	
1590	Stover, Jacob, do.	-	20th Jan. 1815	4	48	

B—Continued.

TENNESSEE—Continued.

No.	Names of decedents, &c.	Rank or grade.	Original commencement of pension.	Pension per month.	Pension per annum.	Remarks, &c.
1591	Sartain, Jacob, *widow*	Private	10th May, 1814	$4 00	$48 00	Widow intermarried, 28th Dec. 1815.
1592	Stout, Isaac, do.	-	28th Jan. -	4	48	
1593	Tucker, Archibald, do.	-	28th Dec. -	4	48	
1594	Tipton, Joshua, do.	-	20th April, 1815	4	48	
1595	Thomas, Mark, do.	-	10th March, -	4	48	
1596	Townsend, Stephen, do.	Sergeant	5th Jan. -	5 50	66	Widow intermarried, 22d Aug. 1815.
1597	Thurman, William, do.	Private	15th Dec. 1814	4	48	
1598	Tannehill, John, do.	-	18th Nov. -	4	48	
1599	Taylor, Thomas, do.	-	20th March, 1813	4	48	
1600	Tarpley, John, do.	-	10th April, 1815	4	48	
1601	Taylor, Absolam, do.	-	21st Jan. -	4	48	
1602	Vaughan, John, do.	-	31st Dec. 1814	4	48	
1603	Viney, Andrew, do.	Sergeant	20th Jan. 1815	5 50	66	
1604	Venable, Richard, do.	Private	26th March, -	4	48	

B—Continued.

TENNESSEE—Continued.

No.	Names of decedents, &c.	Rank or grade.	Original commencement of pension.	Pension per month.	Pension per annum.	Remarks, &c.
1605	Vaught, John, *widow*	Private	24th March, 1815	$ 4 00	$ 48 00	
1606	Van Dyke, Thos. J. do.	Surgeon	27th Dec. 1814	30	360	
1607	Vernon, Neheniah, do.	Artificer of ordnance,				
1608	Vinyard, George, do.	Private	30th April, 1815	8	96	
1609	Wright, William, do.	-	2d May, 1814	4	48	
1610	Williams, Daniel, do.	-	31st Dec. -	4	48	
1611	Walker, John, do.	-	31st Jan. 1815	4	48	
1612	Williams, Benj'n. do.	-	4th May, -	4	48	
1613	Wisenor, Henry, do.	3d lieutenant	18th Jan. -	4	48	
1614	Williams, Wright, do.	Lieut. Colonel	27th Nov. 1814	11 50	138	
1615	Whitsel, Absolem, do.	Corporal	6th May, 1815	30	360	
1616	Woodcock, Wm. do.	Private	11th Jan. 1814	5	60	
1617	Williams, Joseph, do.	-	23d Feb. 1815	4	48	
1618	Wright, Jacob, do.	-	7th Jan. -	4	48	
1619	Walker, Patterson, do.	-	25th Feb. -	4	48	
			26th Feb. -	4	48	

B—Continued.

TENNESSEE—Continued.

No.	Names of decedents, &c.	Rank or grade.	Original commencement of pension,		Pension per month.	Pension per annum.	Remarks, &c.
1620	Whitlock, Wm. *widow*	Private	5th Feb.	1815	$4 00	$48 00	
1621	Willard, Joel, do.	-	27th March, 1814		4	48	
1622	Wear, John, do.	-	29th Jan.	1815	4	48	
1623	Watson, Elijah, do.	-	15th Aug.	-	4	48	
1624	Warham, Thomas, do.	-	12th Feb.	-	4	48	
1625	White, Henry, do.	-	25th Jan.	-	4	48	
1626	Wright, George, do.	-	1st Feb.	-	4	48	
1627	Ward, Eli, do.	-	31st Dec.	1814	4	48	Widow intermarried, 10th July, 1817.
1628	Witherington, Wm. do.	-	8th Feb.	1815	4	48	
1629	White, John, do.	-	15th March, -		4	48	
1630	Warden, John, do.	Corporal	24th Dec.	1814	5	60	
1631	Williams, Hiram, *widow and children*	Private	22d Jan.	-	4	48	Widow intermarried, 2d April, 1815.
1632	Webb, James, *widow*	-	9th Feb.	1815	4	48	

B—Continued.

TENNESSEE—Continued.

No.	Names of decedents, &c.	Rank or grade.	Original commencement of pension.	Pension per month.	Pension per annum.	Remarks, &c.
1633	Walker, Charles, *widow*	Qr. M. Sergeant	20th March, 1815	$6	$72 00	
1634	Wright, Robert, do.	Private	29th Jan. -	4	48	
1635	Walker, William, do.	Corporal	12th Jan. -	5	60	
1636	Webb, Fielding, do.	Private	25th Dec. 1813	4	48	
1637	West, Moses, do.	-	7th Feb. 1815	4	48	
1638	White, Jonathan D. do.	Sergeant	9th April, -	5 50	66	
1639	Whitton, Elijah, do.	Private	21st Nov. 1814	4	48	
1640	York, Abraham, do.	-	9th July, -	4	48	
1641	Yount, Jacob, do.	-	29th March, -	4	48	
1642	Yates, Daniel, do.	-	16th Feb. 1815	4	48	
1643	Yearby, William, do.	-	24th Jan. -	4	48	
					$ 22,762 00	

B—Continued.

LOUISIANA.

No.	Names of decedents, &c.	Rank or grade.	Original commencement of pension.	Pension per month.	Pension per annum.	Remarks, &c.
1644	Johnson, John, *widow*	Private	18th April, 1815	$ 4 00	$ 48	
1645	Shaw, Zacheus, do.	Captain	16th Jan. 1815	20	240 00	
					288	

B—Continued.

INDIANA.

No.	Names of decedents, &c.	Rank or grade.	Original commencement of pension.	Pension per month.	Pension per annum.	Remarks, &c.
1646	Asbury, James, *widow*	Private	7th Nov. 1811	$3 33	$39 96	See act of April 10, 1812
1647	Butner, Edward, *widow and children*		- -	3 33	39 96	Widow intermarried, 26th Sept. 1813. (See also act of April 10. 1812,)
1648	Berry, Thomos, *widow*	1st lt. of riflemen	- -	16 66⅔	200	See act of Apr. 10, 1812.
1649	Clendenin, Thos. do.	Private	- -	3 33	39 96	Do. do. do.
1650	Drummons, John, do.	Sergeant	12th Nov. -	4	48	Do. do. do.
1651	Fisher, Daniel, do.	Private	7th Nov. -	3 33	39 96	Do. do. do.
1652	Hanks, Porter, do.	-	- -	3 33	39 96	Do. do. do.
1653	Hickey, Henry, do.	-	16th July, 1814	3 33	39 96	Do. do. do.
1654	Howell, Adin, do.	-	7th Nov. 1811	4	48	
1655	Kelly, William, do.	-	22d Nov. 1812	3 33	39 96	Do. do.
1656	Lang, John, do.	-		4	48	See act of Mar. 3, 1817.

45

B—Continued.

INDIANA—Continued.

No.	Names of decedents, &c.	Rank or grade.	Original commencement of pension.		Pension per month.	Pension per annum.	Remarks, &c.
1657	Millholland, widow	Corporal	23d Jan.	1814	$5 00	$60 00	See act of Apr. 10, 1812.
1658	Music, Jesse, do.	Private	7th Nov.	1811	3 33	39 96	Do. do. do. do.
1659	M'Coy, John, do.	.	.		3 33	39 96	
1660	McMahon, Richard, do.	1st lieutenant	.		16 $66\frac{2}{3}$	200	Do. do. do. do. (widow intermarried,7th June, 1813.)
1661	Spencer, Spier, do.	Capt. of riflemen	.		25	300	See act of Apr. 10, 1812.
1662	Warrick, Jacob, widow and children	Captain	.		20	240	Do. do. do. (widow intermarried 7th Feb. 1813.)
						1,503 64	

B—Continued.

MISSISSIPPI.

No.	Names of decedents, &c.	Rank or grade.	Original commencement of pension.	Pension per month.	Pension per annum.	Remarks, &c.
1663	Wilkinson, Jas. B. *widow*	Captain	7th Sept. 1813	$ 20 00	$ 240 00	

ILLINOIS TERRITORY.

No.	Names of decedents, &c.	Rank or grade.	Original commencement of pension.	Pension per month.	Pension per annum.	Remarks, &c.
1664	Bezion, Benois, *widow*	Private	22d Nov. 1812	$ 4 00	$ 48 00	
1665	Dunnagan, Isaiah, do.	2d lieutenant	18th Oct. 1813	12 50	150	
1666	Mallett, Joseph, do.	Private	10th Nov. -	4	48	
1667	O'Neal, William, do.	-	18th July, -	4	48	
1668	Rippey, Samuel A. do.	Captain	9th March, 1815	20	240	
1669	Thompson, John B. do.	Corporal	6th Sept. 1814	5	60	
					594 00	

B—Continued.

MISSOURI TERRITORY.

No.	Names of decedents, &c.	Rank or grade.	Original commencement of pension.	Pension per month.	Pension per annum.	Remarks, &c.
1670	Calloway, James,	Captain	7th March, 1815	$ 20 00	$ 240 00	
1671	Covington, Leonard,	Brig. General	11th Nov. 1813	52	624	
					884 00	